Copyright © 2009 Lea Chapin
ISBN-13: 978-1482709254

Celestial Connections
Rev. Lea Chapin
www.CelestialConnections.biz
leachapin@verizon.net

In an effort to present the true and specific information in the context in which it was received, material in this book may seem different form other books as it was dictated, literally, through the author. You may find important principles repeated for emphasis. Please take note. It is suggested you read this book with an open mind and a loving heart, to obtain the greatest level of understanding of these Truth teachings taught by Christ.

Cover design by Puzuzu
Editorial supervision by Julie Haugland
Layout by Wendy Scarpa

First edition printed 2005
Second edition printed 2013
ISBN-13: 978-1482709254

ଈ *Table of Contents* ଔ

Chapters in this book are based on audio transcripts of Christ's teachings as given to me in the year 2003.

ℰᴑ *A Word to the Reader* ᴄ℞

In order to help you understand how I came to receive the Truth teachings from Jesus Christ, I need to tell you how it all began. My passion for doing God's work began early in my life. At the age of 10, I felt as if I was to do "something important" with my life. I did not understand what I felt, I just remember thinking, what is it I am called to do? For many years I wondered and searched, asking myself, what was that elusive feeling all about?

I was born a free spirit, restless, defiant, non-conforming and ever-searching for love and fulfillment in my life. I moved from place to place, not knowing what I was looking for, but I kept searching. Until one day in the spring of 1993, I began to spontaneously hear the words of Spirit. I was receiving a Reiki session from a friend and I remember telling her, "I think I am to receive a message." I began to channel the works of Spirit. I do not remember what I spoke or heard that day, but do remember feeling the presence of spirit in my life. As you can imagine, my life changed dramatically, from that point on. Oh, what a glorious day! I immediately began receiving daily messages from the Angelic Realm. Approximately four years later, I began receiving messages first from the Archangels and then from Christ, the Blessed Mother and Mary Magdalene. Oh, what a surprise and a delight! First, it seemed surreal and I wondered if I was making this up. Could I really be hearing the words of Christ and the Blessed Mother? Why me? I couldn't imagine such powerful and loving beings speaking to me, as I had no religious affiliation and did not attend church. However, I deeply believed and loved God, and had been pursuing spiritual and metaphysical studies for over 10 years. Soon I reconciled my own fears and insecurities, and the daily messages from Christ began. For many years we worked closely together teaching and helping others, both privately and in small group settings.

In the fall of 2003, Christ instructed me that it was time to bring His teachings to the masses. I began to receive these divinely inspired messages clairaudiently. I later transcribed them into paperback and they are available also on CD. These <u>Twelve Mastery Teachings of</u>

Christ are intended for people to truly understand the essence of what He taught over 2,000 years ago. It is my desire that these teachings be shared to awaken the masses and to bring peace to this planet. At the age of 49, I finally understood what I was called to do at the age of 10 which was simply to share the love of Christ's teachings onto the world.

It has been a long journey, but my life purpose and mission is now clear. My passion for Christ's teachings is my life's purpose and my life's mission. I feel blessed and honored each and every day to be a voice for Christ's teachings. As you read this book please allow yourself to receive Christ's teachings in the manner in which they were given: *in love*. Receive His words with an open heart and truly begin to feel the essence of His love. May peace be with you.

Reverend Lea Chapin

ℬ Special Acknowledgments ℭ

My gratitude to Christ, my brother and friend who has blessed and enriched my life with His love, friendship and wisdom, I thank you for your love and presence in my life. I am eternally grateful! Thank you for allowing me the honor of being your voice for Your Truth teachings to be shared with the world.

Don Quillen, my husband and twin flame that has supported me and shared my love for Christ. I thank you and love you dearly.

Marla Wienandt, my dear friend who has helped me to bridge the way for this book to become a reality. I thank you from the bottom of my heart.

Karyn Humphreys and Julie Haugland, thank you for your kindness, generosity, and patience in helping me edit my book. I truly thank you for I could not have done this alone.

Sue Andrews, your willingness to help me from the start of this project will not be forgotten. I thank you from the bottom of my heart.

Other acknowledgements and thanks: Liz Voyles, Kathleen Bashem, June Ziegler, Liz Schultz, Lori Reed, and Linda Mannon. Thank you for your friendships, expertise and support with my work with Great Spirit.

℘ *Introduction* ℘

A message from Christ, Jesus of Nazareth:

I, Christ, Jesus of Nazareth, come forth as a Messenger from God to awaken humanity to their own divinity. My desire is for humanity to reach their true spiritual potential on this Earth plane. I come forth to clarify my teachings as they were not accurately recorded by your historians. I return, as the Living Christ to bring forth the true essence of my teachings in <u>The Twelve Mastery Teachings of Christ</u>. May you embody and embrace my teachings in their fullest essence.

Blessed be to all. May peace be with you.

Jesus Christ

℘ *Lesson of Love* ℘

Welcome and greetings, dearest children. It is I, Christ. I bring forth **Lesson I: the Lesson of Love**. It is imperative, dearest children, that you listen carefully, for this lesson is made with all of you in mind. It is necessary you bring yourselves back into balance with the power of love. It is important you stand in the truth of who you truly are, which is love. Know the energy you bring forth into your vessel was sparked and created by the image of God, for that image is you, that image is love. Mother Earth is the planet of love, you and all the inhabitants of Mother Earth are children of love. As this planet has moved and evolved into its own consciousness, it is necessary each of you move into the consciousness of love, peace and unity.

Dearest children, as I bring these teachings to the earth plane, I will begin with the **Lesson of Love**, and I will end with the **Lesson of Joy**. Joy is the totality of all there is, as love is all-encompassing. These lessons are necessary to help awaken humanity to their own divinity and to awaken humanity to the consciousness of the *true essence of their being*. Humanity has been veiled and has forgotten *who they truly are*. These teachings are brought forth to awaken the masses to the truth of their own divinity. As your soul comes forth within your own life incarnation, within your own life personality, you begin to realize you are more than just your physical being. You are the totality of Great Spirit. As you live in these principles, each of you has a responsibility to yourself, and to the world, to hold and carry these teachings in the name of the Great I Am. My teachings offer much for those who wish to awaken to their own divinity and who wish to understand the principles of Universal Love. My teachings are for all who wish to come forth into the essence and into the totality of *who they truly are*. Allow yourself to be free. Allow yourself to understand the power of love for divine love is all-encompassing and all consuming.

As I taught these principles 2,000 years ago, I bring them forth once again today as the Living Christ. I wish for each of you to live in the principle of love, to live in the vibrational frequency of love, to live in the essence of love, and to live in the power of love. It is time for each of you to come into your own. I wish to tell you, as you stand in the light of the Father, you are love and you are loved. It is necessary for you to bring love into your consciousness even further. Now and forever, you are love and you are loved. Now and forever, you are to bring peace, hope, light and love into your vessel, so you can bring my teachings of love to one another. It has been far too long that this planet and all of humanity has been out of balance and is in need of returning back to the principles of the Great I Am.

It is time for this planet to return back to harmony, balance, peace, love and unity. The Twelve Mastery Teachings that I, Christ, bring forth to you will bring balance and harmony to this planet and to all of humanity. Three-fourths of humanity must return to the principles of **Love, Power, Truth, Oneness, Enlightenment, Forgiveness, Hope, Faith, Rejuvenation, Remembrance, Peace,** and **Joy**. These lessons I bring forth at this time will be felt around the world. The vibrational frequency of these teachings will be felt, as this energy is to be brought forth in a powerful way upon this planet. I wish to bring these teachings to all who are ready to listen, all who are ready to bring forth their own level of light, their own level of love, and the encompassing energy of love and peace upon this planet.

As you breathe in the vibration of love, know the energy of love is what you were created from. Know the vibration of love is all you are. Know the vibration of love is dependent upon nothing. It is not conditional love. It is love from the Father. It is the love you were created from, the love you were sparked from. There is no condition of love, as it is all unconditional. As you begin to feel this within your psyche and within your own physical system, begin to feel this within your own life. Begin to embody this energy of love within your own being; then, and only then, can you spread love out onto the world. As you give your hand to another in love, you give it to yourself. As you give your hand in peace to another, you give it to yourself. As you give your hand in hope to another, you give it to yourself. And so, it is!

As I walked this plane 2,000 years ago bringing the vibrational frequency of love into my own being, I began to live these principles in an embodied spiritual form. This is what I am asking each of you to do on this day. Begin to live these principles in a physical, spiritual form. Dearest children, it is time to move out of your ego and time to move out of your own way. It is time to do the work of the Father. It is time to do what you have come to do: live in love, peace, balance, harmony and joy once again. All I am asking each of you do at this time is to bring your consciousness to' a place of peace, harmony, and balance. I ask you to be at peace, and to live in joy. In simplicity, there is only love.

As I ask you to take a deep breath and to breathe in the vibration and energy of love, fill every cell, every fiber, and every pore of your being with love. Know once again, dearest children, as you breathe in the energy of love, you bring the power of creation through you, and the power of creation within you. As you breathe in this energy, send this energy of love out into the world for all to feel and for all to be healed. For love is healing. The vibration of love is healing. As you extend this love to yourself, extend it to another. Do not hoard this energy, for it is not to be hoarded. The love within you, the creation of love, the image you are, which is love, must be shared. In this light, in this frequency of love is the power of *who you truly are*, you shall find peace. Share, remember, and live in the joy and remembrance of *who you truly are*. Know you are love, and you are loved. As you walk this planet, walk with the confidence that you know who you are. Walk with the confidence that you are loved by all creation; loved by myself, loved by my mother and loved by all of Great Spirit. Feel this vibration within your system as you hold and carry this vibration at a very deep and powerful level within.

So many have forgotten the power of love and have forgotten the feelings of love in its purest form. Many do not understand the *power* of love in its purest form. As you give love to yourself, you give love to another, it changes the world. Love changes all. When you feel the love of a newborn child, you feel the innocence and the purity of love radiating from your heart chakra. This is what you are to feel for yourself, for your brother and your sister. This is what you are to feel for all of humanity and for all of creation, not just a select few. As you walk upon this planet, feel the vibrational frequency of love growing within you each and every day. Begin to embody the energy of love in its purest form which is unconditional love. Never underestimate the power of *who you truly are*, dearest children, for as you grow in the understanding of the love that you are, you will grow into the light frequency of all that you are. You will grow in the frequency of the truth that you are as you begin to value the true essence of *who you truly are*. Only through this then you are free to serve, free to love, and free to be. You are free. You are free. You are free.

Dearest children, let me take you on a journey to a place of pure love and pure light. Deep in the core of your own being is unconditional love. Join me for a moment, and feel this within. Allow your mind to rest. Allow yourself to be taken deep into the crevice where your own spirit resides, where all is at peace, and all is in balance. Bring this energy of love into your consciousness and into your awareness. Allow your mind to relax. Feel yourself quietly melting into the energy and vibration of love. Feel yourself succumbing to this energy and vibration of love. Feel the peace within your heart and the peace within your essence as you journey within. Place your attention at the center of your chest where your physical heart is located. Feel the vibration of love coming from your heart chakra. You are love, and you are loved. Remember that you are created in the image of love. As you begin to feel the vibration of love, hold that love close; first for yourself, and then for another. As you draw this energy close within your frequency and your vibratory field, know the power of love as you begin to feel it within your physical system and within your conscious memory. Live and let live. Allow this energy to come forth in its purest form, for it is truth. It is truth. It is truth.

Live and let live and allow this energy of love to come in its purest form. *Live in joy and remembrance of who you truly are*. Feel the energy of peace as it quietly submerges within your own energy field. Allow your whole body to be bathed with this energy of love, peace, and joy. Feel the frequency of that which you are, which is love. Feel the vibration as you begin to enter into this state of awareness of love. This is what created your own energy field. This is what creates matter into form. As you breathe in the vibration of love, begin to feel this within your heart as you begin to resonate with the power of love.

Dearest children, as you center your attention upon the vibrational frequency of love, feel the power of love, feel the power of light, and feel the power of who you truly are. No one or nothing can take this away. It is your birthright. Carry it, feel it, and know it is sacred. Realize that you were created in the image of the Father, which is love. It is your divine right and your earthly freewill choice to express this love in its purest form. Allow yourself to express this love, first to yourself, and then to another. As you recognize the love vibration in yourself, you recognize it in another. Remember to honor the Christ within yourself and the Christ within another. It is for you to understand to honor the God and the Goddess within as you *live in joy and remembrance of who you truly are.* Feel the sacredness and the power of the vibrational frequency of love. This vibrational frequency is to be felt around the world, for all of humanity and all of creation to feel. These teachings were meant to be brought forth for you to spiritually evolve and grow in the frequency of love. Mother Earth has once again raised her vibrational frequency so that humanity can begin to feel her love so there may be peace, unity and balance on the planet at this time. The Father has brought forth these principles to be taught at this time, for the world to feel, to know, and to live within the truth. Humanity must return to a state of balance and harmony in order for peace to prevail upon Mother Earth. The energy shift in consciousness of 2012 has now heralded in greater peace, love, unity and compassion and the world will now begin to shift into the new vibrational frequency of the divine feminine energy that will truly bring peace to the world.

It is my desire that humanity awaken to the Great I am's principles and I, Christ, have come to share and teach them. I have come to bring love and healing for all who desire to receive my love. Each individual who holds the power of love, who honors it, who recognizes it, and who understands the purity of who they are, can live in the light of which they were created which is the essence of love.

Dearest children, I come to help each of you to understand that the power you hold, the love you hold, and the frequency you hold is, indeed, truth. As you understand the truth from within, you become centered in peace and centered in the calm of knowing that you are love and that you are loved. The vibrational frequency of love is a powerful vibration, much more than you can ever comprehend for the Great Creator's love is immense. If you so choose, I ask you to feel it at the very center of your core and from your heart. Allow yourself to feel it from your mind, heart and soul as it will then embody within every cell, every pore, and every fiber of your being. Know that the truth of who you are is love. Know that the truth of who you are is peace.

I thank you, my children, for your time and your attention. I bring the God's Principles and these Twelve Mastery Teachings to you to help you understand that these are your inherent birthrights as they are the *true essence of my teachings*. At the time of your birth, you were given your spiritual gifts and it is now up to you to awaken them within you. It was always my role to awaken them within you, so you can understand the divinity of who you truly are. I did not come to be your lord and savior. I came only to help bring you peace, love and forgiveness upon your soul. My role as a prophet has been misunderstood, for I did not come to save your sins, for there is nothing to be saved. I ask only that you embody peace, love, forgiveness and joy within your being, for this was my true mission over 2000 years ago and still remains the same.

I truly wish for you to understand that the essence of your love is needed upon this planet to heal this planet and all of humanity. I am asking each of you to reach out to one another, to reach out and to embrace love as the vibrational frequency of love is so desperately needed upon this planet for peace to prevail. Remember, to first bring it to yourself, and then share it with the world. Joy to the world. Joy to the world. Joy to the world. For love, light, hope and freedom are now upon this planet. Peace be with you, my children. Peace be with you. Peace be with you.

And so, it is!

‫ℰ‬ *Lesson of Power* ‫ℛ‬

Dearest children, it is I, Christ. I bring forth **Lesson II: the Lesson of Power**. I ask you, dearest children to open your heart and your mind to the energy of power, for it is the divine power of God within. It is not external power, it is not man-made power; it is the power of love and the divine power of God within. This power is how I used my gifts of healing and manifestation in order to create. I used my God-given power in a way to bring forth what was needed during the time of my ministry. This is what many understand is the power of manifestation. So many people looking outside of themselves seeking power, not understanding that your God-given power is truly within. I simply ask you to look inside of yourself and to examine what your beliefs about power are. Do you place your power in the physical and man-made power? Or do you understand that power comes from connection to God and from within? See where your true intention lies and examine your belief about the use of power. Throughout ages of time, mankind has misused their power and this is the result of the problems that exist upon the Earth at this time. God cannot be blamed for the condition of the Earth and all the maladies, diseases, wars and violence. Nor even the Earth changes that seem to be so prevalent upon your Earth plane at this time. The power of God's divinity is truly within you. It is your choice how you use your power. The divine power of God within you is to be used only with pure intent, not from ego, nor for personal gain, greed, material gain, or for ruling over another. In this power, there is healing, wholeness, balance, and freedom. The power of the divine is love and you were created in the image of that love. It is the power that created you and you have the ability with divine power to create your life as you so choose.

I wish for humanity to understand this principle of power because so many upon your planet have misused their power. This planet has been affected by the misuse of power and Mother Earth has been ravaged due to man's ego, greed, and materialistic gain; in the name of power. Mother Earth has sacrificed herself for all of humanity. Mother Earth has been placed in jeopardy because of man's misuse of power. It is time for each individual to understand your God-given right at birth was the proper use of God's divine power. I, Christ come to help humanity to understand how to live in these Truth teachings and to feel the vibrational frequency of how divine power feels. As you live in the totality of *who you truly are*, begin to understand these teachings and principles as you begin to feel this energy of power within you as the power of the divine.

I ask you simply to begin to breathe in the energy of power. To begin to look deep within your soul and to begin to examine what your belief systems are and at what you understand divine power to be. I ask that you look within and feel the power of the divine within you, as you hold this power within you with the purest of light, the purest of love, and the purest of energy. Go within and understand the power of *who you truly are*, which is love, peace, wholeness, oneness and balance. When I walked this earth plane 2,000 years ago, I brought the energy of love and peace into the lives of those who were ready to listen and this is why I choose to bring my message again in this format. I wish for the readers to understand that my scribe, Reverend Lea Chapin is a messenger of my word and teachings and has been chosen to bring my teachings forth to humanity at this time. Not for personal gain, not for power, but simply because she has chosen to listen and has been a faithful servant onto myself and onto the Father.

I truly wish for you to understand that all of my teachings in this book are encoded with the vibrational frequencies of **Love, Power, Truth, Oneness, Enlightenment, Forgiveness, Hope, Faith, Rejuvenation, Remembrance, Peace** and **Joy**. As you read each teaching, understand that your physical body, mind, soul and soul's essence are truly being encoded and embodied with the power of God's healing, love and peace. As I reiterate, I have chosen to work with Reverend Lea Chapin to bring forth these <u>Twelve Mastery Teachings</u> for all of mankind to know, sense, and embody. I wish for all to embrace the vibrational frequency of power, the power of the divine within. As you feel this power, begin to feel your own strength. No longer do you need to use your own man-made power. No longer do you need to manipulate, be dishonest, greedy, or untruthful. As you hold this power of the divine within, know you are whole and perfect. In perfection, you bring the power of the God within you and stand in the truth of who you truly are. As you stand in the truth of *who you truly are*, you no longer feel afraid. For there is no fear, there is only love. As the power of the divine light within you grows stronger each and every day, begin to feel and understand the level of knowingness from within. As you stand in the truth of *who you truly are*, you begin to realize that there is great freedom and feeling your own sense of divine power. It is not a creation from your own ego, from your own self, but, it is from the God self. It is truth and it is light and it is truly freedom of the soul.

As I have spoken of before, this planet was in dire straights and three-fourths of humanity needed to shift in consciousness in order for Mother Earth to ascend to the next level of evolution. It is now 2013 and Mother Earth has shifted in consciousness and now humanity is in need of catching up with her vibration of love. As we have completed the end of the Mayan calendar in December of 2012, humanity has now risen in consciousness to a new level of understanding that we are all one and we are all connected. With our new technology of the computer and access to the internet, the world has become very small, what one does truly affects another. As our dear friend Kryon who created the unity and peace grid around the planet states, "time is of the essence and there is no time to waste. Each one teach one, each one lead one."

Therefore, God has created a time table for these teachings to come forth to the masses and it is now. As the new energy and consciousness spreads like wildfire for the entire world to embrace, these teachings will become embedded within the conscious and subconscious of each individual. As each individual brings their sense of awareness to these vibrational teachings, the planet can evolve and humanity can evolve as well; but not until.

I, Christ, come to bring these teachings and to help humanity understand these gifts from the Father are your birthright; to help you to understand the true meanings of these truth teachings at this time. As you use your God given power to understand you are connected to the Father, you can tap into the power of the divine within you. This brings clarity, wisdom, and peace to all who wish to listen to the truth within. You are never alone. You are never alone. You are never alone. Understand, dearest children, as you tap into this energy of divine power, you tap into the energy of the four elements: fire, wind, earth and water. Many underestimate the power of the four elements as they are necessary energies that are affecting change upon the planet at this time. These powerful four elements are truly under-rated by humanity in their daily life. For within these powerful energies much is to be received. Simply allow the vibrational frequency of fire to ignite you, wind and water combined with the earth, to ground and stabilize you. In my lifetime, over 2000 years ago, I, my mother, Mary Magdalene and the twelve disciples (both women and men, twelve of each) accessed the four elements to manifest, create, heal and make whole all that was needed for life at that time. Yes, dear ones, there were twelve women disciples. Unheard of in your bible, but indeed, there were twelve women disciples who worked in conjunction with Great Spirit and Mother Earth to help bring forth the balance that we needed in our lives at that time. The twelve women simply taught me the ways of the divine feminine and how to access the power of the earth and the four elements as I moved into becoming the essence of the Christ consciousness into my physical being of Jesus of Nazareth.

Therefore, dearest children, as you move forth into your divine power, please learn to use the four elements to ground and stabilize yourself in order to learn to manifest, create, heal and make whole all that is divinely yours. This will bring you to a new place inside of you that will ignite and allow you to activate the energy of the divine within you.

Dearest children, the physical world and the aspects of your spirit and your soul are all connected. What you do, what you bring forth in the name of God, affects another. What you do in the name of God, if you choose to use it in rightful purpose shall bring forth peace, love, balance and harmony. Please use divine power only for the highest good for all humanity. When you use these principles for the betterment of your own life and for the betterment of mankind, you shall begin to understand the power of God spreads like wildfire. As the earth, wind, fire and water are in balance and harmony with all of creation, it will be for the highest good of each individual to come back into balance and harmony with Mother Earth. Mother Earth is moving rapidly into higher realms of consciousness. Therefore, she is taking another leap into higher consciousness, and now humanity has to catch up with her. As Kryon says, "do you wish to be a part of the problem, or do you wish to be a part of the solution?" Simply meaning, these principles are being taught for humanity to move their consciousness into a new state of peace and love in order to match the vibrational frequency and consciousness of Mother Earth.

Dearest children of the light, do not be afraid to change your consciousness from a limited mental mind to an opening and loving spiritual mind in order to bring love and peace into your own life and onto the world. When you make a conscious decision to live in peace, harmony, and faith, you have reclaimed the truth of *who you truly are*. Each and every day, you are to understand the power of *who you truly are*. Each and every day, you are to understand you are love and you are loved. When you misuse your power, there are repercussions on a spirit and soul level, therefore, your soul will limit your ability to ascend into higher spiritual consciousness. When you use your divine power for the highest good for all concerned, then you become one with the Father. Allow these principles to be the principles by which you live. Let go and let God. Let go and let God.

Dearest children, as I stand before you, I send you my own divine power, which is the power of love which is the power from the Father. As I come forth as the Living Christ, I anoint you with the power of the Christ Consciousness which shall allow you to open to your higher self, to the true essence of *who you truly are*. As you become the awakened Christ, as you become a lighted being of the Christ, use this power for only good and with pure intention. For this is how you begin to use and access this vibrational frequency of divine power. There is softness and peace within this power for it is the power of the divine feminine which is love, peace, compassion and mercy. And yet, there is strength. The divine feminine energy is truly embodied in the energy of my mother who truly represents the power of the divine. Understand that the use of this power of the divine is your birthright. You are being awakened to these truth principles, and the veils are being lifted; as the remembrance of *who you truly are* comes forth. Understand you are never alone. You are never alone. You are never alone.

As I take my leave, I place my hand upon your heart and upon your throat chakra. I ask you to use God's power through your vocal cords to speak and spread the energy of love. The power I speak of is the energy of the divine within you. The use of divine power can create, manifest and make whole all that is yours. Dearest children, breathe in this vibrational frequency of divine power as it becomes centered within your heart chakra and vibrates within your throat chakra and throughout your being. Allow it to come down through the crown chakra and allow it to connect into the Earth Star chakra within your feet and intentionally connect yourself to the crystalline core of Mother Earth. There you are grounded in the power of the Father, and the power of the Mother and in the totality of *who you truly are*. As you stand in your own divine power, you stand in truth, light, and love. I thank you, dear children. I love you, and I pray you awaken to these truth teachings and to your own divine power within. It is time for this planet and all of humanity to awaken to the divinity of the power of God and all these teachings that epitomize the Father's principles of love. I thank you, my children. I honor you, and I send you peace. Go within and discover the divine power, which is love and light from within. Go within. Go within. Go within.

And so, it is!

⅏ Lesson of Truth ⅏

Dearest children, it is I, Christ. I bring forth **Lesson III: the Lesson of Truth**. I ask you to understand that all of my truth teachings are embodied with love. As a messenger of God's word, it was the energy of truth that resonated within my own soul in my mission as I spoke the truth as I knew it. My desire was to awaken all souls to the truth of their own divinity. Today, as the Living Christ, I am committed to seeking truth for the betterment of mankind. The first lesson, the Lesson of Love is the bridge to bringing forth the remaining lessons.

The essence of the Lesson of Love will come forth in the remembrance of truth. When the world was created, there was truth. In all of life, there is truth. In every cell, every fiber, and every pore of your being, you were created from truth, and in truth resides the essence of love. The power of love, the creation of the Father, lives within you. Within you is the truth of all you are, you are truly a divine being.

God has brought forth the **Lesson of Truth**, for you to remember that you were created in truth. Dearest children, do not underestimate the power God has given you. Within every cell, every fiber, every pore of your being, you hold all of God's principles within. You hold the principle of divine love and the principle and vibration of power, as well as the principles and vibration of divine truth, as you hold the other nine lessons, as well. In this vibrational frequency of truth, it is your wisdom, your knowledge, your innate connection to the divine within you that is known as truth.

These teachings are called truth teachings, for they are principles from the Father. Yes, it is I, Christ, Jesus of Nazareth. I have been chosen to bring these truth teachings from God through the vessel called Lea. I wish for you to understand the truth that you are and the essence of that truth is your birthright. Truth is the highest teaching, the highest oneness, the highest knowingness, and the gift given unto mankind from the Father. Of all these teachings, it is truth that shall prevail within each of you as your birthright. Truth is what resonates within your very core; therefore, when you hear truth, you just know it. There is no explanation as there is only knowingness for the truth of knowingness comes from deep within the soul. This is the gift God has given each of you to use as discernment, as a compass for you to discern the decisions you need to make here on planet Earth. This Lesson of Truth and these truth teachings are given to you out of love by the Great I Am. In this energy of truth, you hold and carry the power of knowingness, power of oneness, and indeed, hold and carry the power of love.

Two thousand years ago when I, Christ, brought forth these truth teachings in the manner in which I taught, there was much rejection and much skepticism, as well as much bitterness, anger and hatred. For you see, mankind in that time did not understand the power of God within them. Yes, I had many followers who felt the energy of truth as they used their own discernment and listened from their heart. This is how truth is felt, for this is how you know what truth is. It is felt within your heart, your soul, and within your soul's essence. Do not underestimate the power of *who you truly are*. Do not underestimate the power of the light that you are for each of you were created in truth in the image of God. Do not underestimate the being of truth that you are. You are God. Yes, dearest children you are God. God resides within you. Within every cell, every fiber, and every pore of your being, you are God. This truth, this knowingness, is the truth of God within you. Many look to others seeking their truth. Many look outside of themselves for their truth. Many look to their religion for truth. I am not suggesting that religion has no place in seeking your truth, but I simply ask you to truly look within and seek your own truth as it resonates with your own soul. Truth comes from within. Each individual has their own innate wisdom, as truth is your divine birthright. So I ask you to be still and allow the silence from within be your guide for your own knowingness and truth.

In truth, remember your divinity and remember your power. Remember you are love and you are light. In truth, you hold within every cell, ever fiber, and every pore of your being, you radiate the energy of God. As you embody the presence of the God within you, God only asks you speak the truth within you with the purest of intentions, the purest of love, and the purest of light that you can hold and carry within your system. For in truth, you stand in the vibration of love and you stand in the remembrance of *who you truly are*. In truth, you hold these teachings of the Father within you, for the truth within you lies within your soul. Live in joy and remembrance of *who you truly are*. It lies within the remembrance of that which you are created from, which is the spark of God, which is the image of light within you.

As I bring forth these teachings, I ask humanity to understand that truth is not outside of you. You do not have to look to another for your own truth, to find God, to look to another to find your connection to the divine, for it is inside of you. If you choose to go to your house of worship that is fine and well; however, dearest children, your connection to God is within. No structure, no religion, no minister, no priest, no rabbi; is your connection to truth. The truth is within you, and you are connected to God. This is what I wished to tell the people 2,000 years ago, and what I wish to tell them again today. Who you are, what you know, and your connection to the divine; is within you. Do not go outside of yourself to seek answers, but turn within. Quietly turn within and find the truth. Listen to your heart and listen to your intuition. Listen to the stirrings within your own soul and within your own soul's essence. Listen to the inner voice within you that tells you your own truth.

When you search outside of yourself for answers and look to others to bring you truth, you are discounting your connection to your own divine, therefore you are separating yourself from your connection to God. Dearest children, separation is only an illusion, for you already are connected as you were connected at your birth. This is what I am trying to tell you, dearest ones. You already are connected to God, for separation is only an illusion as we all are connected as one light, one love, one energy. Yes, dearest children, when you feel disconnected from God and refuse to listen, you may feel alone and separate, but it is only an illusion. You always are connected; however, you have the responsibility, the free will choice, to listen to your own still, quiet voice from within, if you so choose. All you have to do is ask and you shall receive, for you have never lost your connection. Simply turn within. Listen to the small voice within. Listen to the stirrings of your soul from deep within. I come to teach you to look within, to clear out your mind, to clear out your body so you can listen carefully to what you are to do with your life. As you listen, shall you be connected to your soul's purpose and everything in your life can be your guide.

Each individual has their own divine pathway. Each individual has their own divine mission. Your truth is different from another's truth, but it is all one truth. This is why *it is not for you to judge another's truth because that is right and true for them.* I simply ask to you place no judgment upon another's knowingness/truth as their connection to the divine is simply theirs and theirs alone. How can there be different truths, you ask? For again, dearest children, there is only oneness, for we are all one and we are all connected. It is not different. It is only a separate experience for each individual; however, it is all the same, for it is all connected to the divine. Listen carefully to the words of another. For, there lies the energy of God. By the mere breath and the vibration of your speech, by the vibration of your own vocal cords bringing forth the messages from within, there resides truth. For within every word you speak, there is the vibration of love from God. Through your mere breath, through your mere existence, you are truth, you are love as your are a divine child of God. Dearest children, know the greatest gift the Great Creator has given you is your ability to discern the truth. The greatest gift you can give yourself is beginning to listen to know you are truth and you have been given this gift of truth from the Father. Dearest children, as I have said your individual truths are not separate for they are all one with the Father. Therefore, do not separate yourself from another because they have a different religion or different belief system, or a different color of skin, for this will only cause separation and fear, anger and loneliness. Simply understand that all your earthly and galactic brothers and sisters are connected in oneness and each being holds the energy of God's truth deep within their essence. Every individual who lives on this planet holds and carries the truth of the Father within them, and there is no separation in truth, there is only power and love. God wishes for you to know there is not to be separation. As separation is what creates war and violence, separation is what keeps individuals from being peaceful on planet Earth. It is time now that humanity come together in unity, peace, love and harmony for this is how peace shall prevail on the planet, one person at a time taking responsibility for their own actions, words and deeds.

Dearest children, understand and accept your earthly brothers and sisters for who they truly are. Remember you are all the same. There is no difference in race, creed, color, or religion. For there is no difference, you are all the same. You are all one, created in the truth, the love, and the power of the Father. This is what I came to teach you. This is what I came to bring you. This is what I came to help you to understand. You all are one, you are the truth, the way and the light. Dearest children, understand there is no difference between you, only an illusion of separation amongst you that keeps you separate from one another, and keeps you in fear of one another. This is not what God intended for this planet. God intended this planet to be of love and peace. As planet Earth has ascended into higher consciousness, there will be no place for fear, greed or violence. Humanity can no longer afford to remain selfish and separate from one another. The state of the world is such that fear and separation is prevalent and we are pleased that humanity is now willing to take a stand and speak their truth against violence and human suffering. This is why many of the governments around the globe are crumbling as their ideologies have been based on greed and serving only a select few. I applaud humanity for standing up for truth and bringing justice and unity to the forefront. Simply, that which is truth will be brought forth and recognized and that which is not of truth will be exposed and fall away.

God has decreed peace for this planet for planet Earth is the planet of love. God is bringing peace to this planet, as I speak. These next few years are powerful years of heralding peace upon planet Earth. All individuals who choose truth, who choose to understand they are not separate from their earthly/galactic brothers and sisters, will begin to feel peace and embody peace into their being. As you look at your earthly brothers and sisters as an extension of yourself, know that what he or she says, how they act or how they behave is their own truth. Do not judge them and do not keep yourself separate from them. This is not what the Father intended, not what he desires for any of you, to be separate. You were created in love and you were created in the image of the divine truth of the Father. This is a powerful vibrational frequency you each hold and carry. You cannot move forward in your own awakening and in your enlightenment until you realize, dearest children, that you are truth. As you hold truth within you, know it is your birthright from the Father. The vibrational frequency of truth is encoded within your etheric blueprint and into your physical DNA. As you allow yourself to feel the love and peace of truth, then there shall be no separation between you and another.

The destiny for planet Earth and all of humanity is moving forward into the energy of truth, peace and love. Dearest children, all individuals, all institutions, who are not of truth will be exposed, for truth shall prevail. This planet will be a peaceful planet as it was intended. God has decreed that no one shall continue to further hurt planet Earth. No being will be allowed to reign upon this planet that has war and hatred, fear and anger within their heart. This seems impossible to you, but it is not! The Father has decreed this planet to be the planet of peace, love, and unity, and it shall be. Those individuals who cannot hold and carry the vibration of peace and love will leave this planet and move into another dimension, another place and time, which is suitable to their vibration. No one will be left on this planet that is not in balance and harmony with Mother Earth and with God's truth teachings. This planet is in the last 10,000 year cycle of its evolution. At the end of the 10,000 year cycle, only gentle and loving beings will be allowed to live on planet Earth as it is its destiny.

This, you say, cannot be. This, you say, is impossible. All things are possible through God. Planet Earth's destiny is to return back to its original state of peace, love, harmony and balance. Remember, it begins with one person at a time. Each one teach one, each one lead one. As you hold and carry the energy and vibrations of all these teachings from love to joy there you shall embody peace, be peace and live peace.

All of these teachings are your birthright. These teachings are ingrained within you so deeply even when you stop to ponder a moment and look within your heart, you know truth prevails. Feel the energy of truth within you. Truth is love and truth is divine power. Truth is the devotion and the connection to the divine within you. Can you feel it? Can you hear it? Can you listen to the stirrings within you? Are you encouraged, or are you afraid? Use your time to listen to the inner stirrings of your own truth. Stand in your power and in the knowingness of who you truly are.

The Twelve Mastery Teachings of Christ each hold a powerful vibrational frequency of healing and love. Once again, dearest children, do not create separation between you and your earthly brother or you and your earthly sister because of what you believe is not truth. Many may not understand my teachings in this book as truth, but please keep an open heart and an open mind. For, it is all truth. This book was created in love as it was given to you from God, as He loves you deeply. Know and understand, dearest children, as you stand in these teachings and live in your truth, you are the image of the divine and, in this, there is power and peace. In this, you find the tranquility you have been searching for. In this, you know you are at home. Home is where the heart is and home is the birthright to your connection to the divine. Your home is the God within you. All that resides within your being is love, peace, joy, remembrance, wisdom, and light. You are created and have been given all these gifts, the fruits of the spirit, from the Father. When you settle into this knowingness of the truth of who you are, that you are a divine God and a divine Goddess, then you can *live in the remembrance and the joy of who you truly are*. Indeed, you shall live in the truth of which you were created and, in this, you shall find peace.

Dearest children, I ask you to understand there is no separation between you and another. There is only truth. For truth is the connection between you and another. Truth is the connection between you and God. Remember, dearest children, truth cannot be from outside of yourself, for it lies within your soul and within your soul's essence. The soul resides near your heart. This is where you feel love and where you feel the divinity of the Father within you. Home is where the heart is. Your home is the soul that resonates to the truth of your being. Go now, dearest children, in the truth, the love, and the understanding of who you truly are. Never be afraid. Only be at peace. I thank you, my children, and I take my leave. I thank you for all you bring forth in the name of the Great I Am. Live in the truth of who you are. Live in the light of which you are created. Go in peace, my children. Go in peace. Go in peace. Go in peace.

And so, it is!

ℬ *Lesson of Oneness* ℭ

Dearest children, it is I, Christ. I bring forth **Lesson IV, the Lesson of Oneness**. This lesson is about your connection to the divine. It is about your connection to all you are. Every cell, every pore, every fiber of your being is connected to oneness. However, you have forgotten your connection to your own divinity. You have forgotten your own connection to oneness. There were many veils that were placed over you at your birth. It is your free will choice to awaken and allow these veils to be lifted one by one by one as you begin to *live in the joy and remembrance of who you truly are.* It is your connection to God that is your birthright. It is your connection to the divine that is your God-given right. At the time of your inception, you were sparked with the image and the creation of the divine. With each successive lifetime, with each incarnation, with each remembrance of the totality of who you truly are, you draw closer to oneness as your birthright.

On this day, we begin to lift the veils of remembrance so you may begin to connect to the energy of oneness. Therefore, you shall begin to feel the joy, feel the love and feel the connection to the divinity of who you truly are. As God has given you this gift of remembrance you may choose to awaken to your own divinity, hence embracing the energy of oneness. God has given you free will choice, consequently, it is always your choice if you choose to awaken or to remain veiled. You were created in light, and light is one, one with the Father and one with all. Each soul/spirit who came to planet Earth was selected at the Great Conclave to bring their brilliant light to planet Earth. As we are all beings of light, and were all created in the image of the Father, we are all connected to the totality of all there is. All here on Earth at this time, simply are here for purpose and good and the great Lesson of Oneness is truly a gift to remember, embrace and embody.

What I, Christ, mean by this, dearest children is that you are to live in the image of God, as you were destined and created to be. You have forgotten who you are out of your own fear, out of your own lack of awareness. Dearest children, it is time to understand it is your God-given right; it is your birthright, to be connected to the divine and to live as a spiritual being in your physical embodiment on this earth plane. For heaven is on earth. It is not outside of you. It is within you.

You are one with the divine Father, and one with the divine Mother, and one with all of creation. I ask you, dearest children, to set aside any worries you have, step back for a moment and allow yourselves to feel this energy of oneness. Allow yourself to feel the energy move from the tips of your fingers to the soles of your feet as it resonates throughout your physical and energetic system. There, you shall begin to feel this vibration as it is the oneness and the totality of *who you truly are*. As you allow the energy of oneness to connect and open throughout your chakras, realize this is the connection to your own divinity. Dearest children, allow yourself to feel this energy of God and Goddess residing within you for in this is where you shall find peace. As you allow yourself to connect to the energy of oneness, reconnect to the memory that has been veiled from you *of who you truly are*. Take a deep breath and allow the energy to resonate through your system. Feel the energy of oneness for it is the energy of the divine within you. As you reclaim your divinity, as you reclaim your oneness, understand the power, and love you hold, is the energy of oneness. You are a God. You are a Goddess. Your body is a temple of God. As you embody the energy of God and Goddess within you, you are free. Free to love, free to be, and free to live in the totality of all that you are.

Take another deep breath and feel the energy pulsating into your fingertips as you begin to feel the connection to the divine. Allow yourself to have this re-awakening. As you allow your hands to tingle with the power of God's warmth, begin to realize the power of God is within you. Dearest children, feel the realization of the God/Goddess energy within your fingertips. Feel the energy as it begins to activate and move into your heart chakra. Feel the sensation of this movement as it allows you to awaken to the truth and to the totality of all that you are. Many have forgotten who they truly are, as many have misunderstood who they truly are. As you reconnect to the energy of oneness, you shall find peace and tranquility upon your soul and soul's essence. Allow yourself to be in a state of peace, as you center yourself in the truth of your divine power, which is love. It is not power outside of you; it is the divine power of the God within. It is the true power that lives and vibrates within every cell, every pore, and every fiber of your body. It is the power that is connected to the divine. As you use the power of the God source within you to re-awaken, you shall begin to feel this energy vibrating through your system. Feel this exhilaration and this excitement as you connect deeper to God within. Take another deep breath and allow yourself to be free. Free to love. Free to love. Free to love.

I ask you dearest children, never underestimate the power of who you truly are, as you are truly divine. As you walk upon this earth plane, do not walk in arrogance, walk in confidence. Walk in the respect of the knowingness that you are a divine child of God. As you begin to awaken to oneness, begin to have greater understanding of *who you truly are.* You are connected to God and all is good. It is when you become separated in your mind and heart that you shall become separate from God. So many individuals are suffering as they have become separated from God, hence feeling fear, pain, anger and lack. This level of separation is simply the disconnection to your own divinity. Many blame God for their pain and suffering and misunderstand that each individual is responsible for their own level of physical, mental, emotional and spiritual well-being.

God is not to blame for neither your pain nor is responsible for your happiness. Each soul is simply responsible for they are the co-creators of their own life with the divine. The divine is within you, for every cell, every pore, every fiber of your being is God. Every inch of your body is God. Every thought you have is empowered with the energy of God and Goddess. Every action, word, deed, thought or intent you have is encoded with the divine. This encoding can be used for good, or it can be used for what many call misdirection. It is with your intent to use the divinity within you that can assist you on becoming stronger in your connection to oneness each and every day. As you recognize your own divinity, recognize it in another. As you recognize the Christ within Me, recognize the Christ within yourself. There is no separation, there is only oneness. Prejudice, fear, bigotry, bias, judgment and hatred are false emotions, as they are ruled by fear, not by love. This is what keeps each one separate from another. These negative emotions, these belief systems, all stem from fear and disconnection from the Father. As you begin to feel this energy vibrating within your finger tips and throughout your system, know you are one with the Father. As you begin feel this energy within, know you are vibrating to the energy of oneness.

Many upon your planet have separated themselves from God because of their own mind and what they believe is rationality, practicality, scientific proof or just plain good old common sense. As you begin to feel the energy of oneness within you, this has nothing to do with the mental mind or ego. Your connection to the divine has nothing to do with practicality or with good old common sense. It is the knowingness of living and embodying the energy within you as the divine you are. There may be many who come to you, wanting to know the proof of God, you are to rest assured, and tell them that their mere presence, is the embodiment and evidence of the image of God.

Dearest children, much has been given upon the evidence and the proof of God throughout history and throughout time, however, you are connected by your mere existence, by your mere presence. The miracle of a new born baby in its purest form is the essence of God which is simply love. For do not all love new life? Do not all love the innocence and purity of new life? Have you forgotten that you, too, are connected to God by every cell, every pore, and every fiber of your being? As you walk upon Mother Earth, feel the energy of the divine within you, and know God resonates fully within. Know you are in perfect health, perfect radiance, and perfect oneness with the Father. Every aspect of your life is in divine order. Yes, you have freewill choice, but every step of the way you are living in divine order. There are crossroads and pathways to be taken and challenges to be met, but know, dearest children, all is in divine order and all is as it should be. As you realize and begin to understand that life is connected by the energy of the one light, one love, then you now can being to understand that you are not separate from the energy, only separate by your mere thought; only separate by your mere belief; only separate by of your own fear.

Dearest children, realize there is no need to be afraid, for God is alive and well within you and you are well connected to the energy of oneness. Be still and know that you are God. God is alive and well within you and directing your life each and every day. No one or nothing can change this. It is truth. Just as you believe in my image as the Christ who walked upon this planet 2,000 years ago. I am alive and well. My energy is here, present for you, speaking to you at this time. I tell you, dearest children, what I wished to teach 2,000 years ago; I bring forth again in these teachings to awaken humanity to the truth of

God' principles. The first lesson is love and the last lesson is joy. The most important lesson is oneness. Remember you are one with the Father.

Dearest children, the **Lesson of Oneness** is so important for you to feel, truly feel, the energy of God in every cell, every pore, and every fiber of your being. This is why I am asking each of you to begin to feel the energy of oneness vibrating through the tips of your finger to the bottoms of your feet so you may have full sensory perception and a sense within yourself that God is real. For those doubting Thomases who question God's presence in their lives, the energy of God within their own being is proof within it self. As you read these teachings understand that they are potent and powerful and they are encoded with my love. I, Christ, am the messenger bringing these lessons unto you at this time. It is necessary that each individual upon this planet begin to find their oneness, to find their reconnection to the Father, to begin to be drawn towards the light of the Father. It is of the utmost importance each person awakens to their own divinity; because this planet has shifted her consciousness into a new vibrational frequency of love and peace. These lessons are brought forth out onto the world so humanity can truly understand God's truth principles.

Dearest children, it may not seem pertinent to you to understand and embody these Twelve Mastery Teachings of Christ at this time, however, if you wish to awaken to the divinity within you, you will listen and you will learn. I do not wish to admonish you, but I wish to tell you time is of the essence. We have much to do and there is much to teach upon this earth plane, as there are many to reach and many to help. Many souls do not remember they are connected to the divine, therefore their souls are lost, angry, fearful, and in pain. There is no need for any such emotion. There is only need for peace, love, and joy.

I, Christ, Jesus of Nazareth, wish to bring forth these Twelve Mastery Teachings to help humanity reconnect to oneness. These teachings are designed to reconnect all beings to their own divinity. It is imperative and important each soul awaken to the light and the love of the Father and release their veils of forgetfulness. Open your heart to the energy of love, peace, joy, and remembrance of *who you truly are*. Begin to feel the energizing movement of oneness within you. Feel the passion of your life's purpose and begin to feel the connection to the divinity within you. Time is precious and the time to re-awaken is now. As Kryon says, "there is no time to waste," for there is only love to be brought forth.

Dearest children, begin to open your heart to these truth teachings, and allow the energy of love to fill your mind, body and soul with peace, love, balance and harmony. As your open your heart you will begin to feel the oneness and the love of the Father within your system so strongly you will be full of love and joy. May you a allow your fear to be released and your anger to be extinguished. Allow the joy and the remembrance of *who you truly are* to embody and embrace you in love. You are truly blessed with love from the Father which is encoded within every cell, every fiber, and every pore of your being. As I speak, every cell in your body is being encoded with God's love. Please allow every cell to be awakened to love, for God is love. Love is the totality of oneness. Love is all there is. As your body begins to vibrate to the energy of love, you shall begin to vibrate to the energy of God. You and the Father are one. Let go and let God. You and the Father are one. Let go and let God. Allow your beautiful light to shine and know the truth of who you are. Allow yourself to feel the essence of your being. Feel the joy, as you are truly children of the light. You truly are children of the divine. Rest in the knowledge that you are one with the Father, and you are one with all of creation. You are one with all there is. There is no more separation. There is no more fear. There is no more violence. There is only love.

Dearest children, as I take my leave, I bless you. I honor you and I bestow this gift of oneness upon your soul and upon your soul's essence so you will awaken to the divinity of who you truly are. I thank you, my children. I honor you. I bless you, and I send my peace.

And so, it is!

ഇ *Lesson of Enlightenment* ぬ

Dearest children, it is I, Christ. I bring forth **Lesson V, the Lesson of Enlightenment**. It is about enlightening yourself to further knowledge and development in the energy of the Father. This energy is about expansion and it is about change. It is about allowing the energy within you to shift, change, and grow. As Kryon says, "time is of the essence, there is no time to waste." As you have been told, this energy of change and this Energy of Enlightenment are about bringing forth the energy of truth, love, and light into your being. When you become enlightened, it takes courage to change and to move forward. It takes courage to let go of the past that no longer serves you. Let go and let God. Those who have remain "stuck" in their old behaviors & belief systems will soon find it necessary to shift out of the old patriarchal energy which is anger, fear, violence, greed and capitalistic gain. The new energies that have emerged on the planet as of 2012, are truly the energy of the Divine Feminine, simply meaning it is an energy of peace, love, unity, harmony and balance. Simply we are all one and what effects one, effects another. The energy of the Divine Feminine is truly about peace. Mother Earth is in her final stage of her ascension process as she was created to be the planet of love and peace.

Understand these new energies are bringing swift changes throughout Mother Earth. The immense amount of Earth changes upon the planet are not meant to frighten or cause mankind misery or pain. Mother Earth is a living, breathing entity such as you. It is for you to understand it is not her intention to hurt or cause harm to her children who reside upon this planet. Mother Earth simply wishes for you to understand that she, too, is suffering due to humanity's lack of respect for her and her resources. When the Earth changes do occur, Mother Earth also feels deep pain, as well. For she must rid herself of the negativity that humanity has emitted into the ethers and on the surface of her back. Billions of souls are discharging their own emotional pain thus creating a collective consciousness of negativity upon the planet. Understand that Mother Earth, as I've said, does not wish to harm, but she must clear the negative energy that builds up from her own being. Just as you need to clear your own emotions, she is in need of doing the same. Therefore, it is important that each individual become enlightened and responsible for their own mental and emotional wellbeing. Each time the soul discharges negativity, where do you think it goes? Have you ever thought how it affects another or even that it is emitted into the ethers and Mother Earth is absorbing it?

This **Lesson of Enlightenment** is a necessary lesson as a part of humanity's growth towards ascension. As you take responsibility for understanding that you are connected to all of creation, including Mother Earth, your behaviors, your actions, your words and deeds are indeed affecting Mother Earth more than you could ever realize. As you make a choice to become enlightened, this shall bring you closer to God. This evolutionary change and enlightenment will bring humanity closer to God, as each soul awakens to their own divinity. Those who do not understand this, will be caught up in their own fear, be caught up in their own illusion, and be caught up in their separateness from God. Again, this energy is not to frighten, the purpose is to bring love, harmony, and balance to humanity and to Mother Earth. The divine feminine, which is truly the energy of enlightenment, will awaken all who choose to be seeded with the beautiful energy of God's healing love and light. For enlightenment, shall bring forth calmness and an understanding that all is in divine order and all is as it should be. The many souls who have lost their lives during Earth changes, natural disasters and acts of violence did not sacrifice their lives in vain. Many of these souls are highly evolved beings who have sacrificed their physical lives for a greater purpose. It is imperative to understand, these sacrifices were sacrifices of LOVE. These souls are to be commended, for they are highly evolved souls, who chose to give their life to help humanity to return back to the principles of love from the Father. Dearest children, you must not use these tragedies for your own personal gain, for these lost lives are sacred. They gave their life in love and it is this love that will bring peace, balance, and harmony to planet Earth and all of creation.

Each new day is an opportunity of great growth, an opportunity to bring joy, love, peace, and enlightenment to the world. Those who hold the love, light and peace within them will be the ones who will bring forth the higher conscious energies upon the planet at this time. The new energies have many names, the Age of Enlightenment, the Age of Aquarius, the Rebirth of the Divine Feminine, the Golden Age. There are many light-workers, missionaries and way showers of the light who are working on behalf of the ascension process for both

Mother Earth and humanity to ascend to the next level of evolutionary consciousness. My <u>Twelve Mastery Teachings of Christ</u> are simply to help the masses begin to understand they are not to live in fear regarding this new age of enlightenment as in doing so they shall create separation from the Great I Am. Humanity must understand change is constant and all change is in divine order. Understand, dearest children you are no longer to fear what you do not understand. Be not afraid of Earth's evolutionary changes, as they are a natural part of life. Mother Earth is constantly evolving and changing. Many believed that the world was going to come to an end at the end of the Mayan calendar of December 21, 2012. It is for you to understand the world did come to an end, but not physically. The consciousness of the planet did shift into higher consciousness of love, peace, unity and harmony for all the world to feel, to see and to know.

As you trust in the faith of God and these new energies upon the planet, may you trust in the energy of your own divinity. Simply begin to awaken to the truth, the way and the light that guides like a compass. Dearest ones, I ask each of you to teach and lead the masses regarding this **Lesson of Enlightenment**. There are many enlightened beings bringing this message of peace and love to this planet. *As I, Christ, was the messenger bringing this message 2000 years ago, I continue to bring this message again today and will continue to bring it until the world finally rests in peace.* As humanity begins to listen to their own still, quiet voice within and open their hearts to love, then one can truly feel the energy of enlightenment upon their soul and their soul's essence. Each one teach one, each one lead one and this is how truth and enlightenment shall prevail upon the planet.

The **Lesson of Enlightenment** is simply about moving forward into the soul's journey into ascension. Many may not understand the ascension process. It simply takes a conscious focus and a willing mind to accept that change is constant. Simply begin to allow yourself to change and shift your consciousness into a state of enlightenment for peace and balance. All of you have certain behavioral patterns that no longer serve you and are self-sabotaging. It is your choice each day if you wish to remain stubborn and live from your ego or simply learn to relax, let go and let God and allow your beautiful light to shine. As you begin to let go and let God, the freedom and the joy of living again as an enlightened being shall come forth. Dearest children, as you move forward in this journey of enlightenment, understand change is necessary and change is constant. The fear people hold onto so tightly within themselves, is a part of their own sense of isolation and feeling of separation from God. Each soul has free will choice to move forward into the new evolutionary process that is occurring on the planet at this time This planet is in dire need of clearing and it begins with one soul at a time. I ask each of you to release your fear and resistance to change in order for personal and planetary ascension to occur. Each soul has the power to change the lives with the power of God's truth principles.

Dearest children, it is necessary for humanity to understand that you are co-creators with God. Each of you are the captains of your own ship, with God and your own angelic team by your side. Allow yourself to understand the love you hold within your being, within your own presence, is of great light, love, hope, and joy. It is necessary each being bring love and peace from within as love heals all. It is my desire that each being embrace these new energies of love, peace and enlightenment so all beings can hold and carry peace and the light of God within every cell, every fiber, and every pore of their being.

Dearest ones, the **Lesson of Enlightenment** is about bringing forth the energy of change and allowance and moving forward into a new level of understanding that we are all one and we are all connected. When you come to accept this, when you come to understand this, when you come to embrace this, there is truth and you become empowered by your knowingness with your connection to God. This is where hope, faith and courage play a major role in your spiritual growth and development. As you develop these attributes then you shall move forward into your own evolutionary process of enlightenment. Many have misunderstood the true meaning of the word ascension. Many feel they will move out of their physical bodies and then ascend into the heavens. No! True ascension is the enlightenment process as it is the enlightenment of the heart, mind, and soul. There is a false perception that I, Christ will return and you will be taken back into the heavens. No! This is not truth and will not occur. True ascension is an evolutionary process, a journey of the soul. It is the soul's journey. It is the journey of Mother Earth and humanity's contract return to a state of peace, harmony, balance and unity. Please have the courage to move into the journey of enlightenment, despite resistance, fear of pain and change, and regardless of the inconveniences it may cause you. Then and only then will you gain in love, in the connection to the Father. This is truly the ascension of which so many speak.

Dearest children, I pray all will awaken to their own enlightenment as the celestial realm and your galactic brothers and sisters continue to assist planet Earth and all of humanity in returning back to God in their full enlightenment. We thank you, dearest children, for being willing to embrace the Lesson of Enlightenment so that peace may prevail. We are ever so grateful for your level of commitment and love. Go in peace. Go in light. Go in truth.

And so, it is!

⁊ *Lesson of Forgiveness* ⳍ

Dearest children, it is I, Christ. I bring forth **Lesson VI: the Lesson of Forgiveness**. I ask you to place your feet firmly upon the ground and begin to breathe in the energy of the wind, earth, water, and fire. As you bring the energy of the four elements into your being, begin to open to the energy of Forgiveness. This **Lesson of Forgiveness** is extremely powerful and is one if great magnitude. As you breathe in the energy of love which has been given to you, and as you breathe in the energy of oneness which has been bestowed upon you, breathe in the energy of your own divine power and the power of the Great I Am.

Dearest children, it is truly an exemplary being who understand this **Lesson of Forgiveness** for it is the hardest lesson of all to learn. As I help you to understand the power of love and forgiveness, the power of love and forgiveness will heal all. As we have spoken about the power of unconditional love, it is most important to understand that as you begin to embody unconditional love into your being in its fullest, there you can begin to learn to forgive. As I lay upon the cross, my message to all was simply, "forgive them, for they know not what they do". As much as I physically suffered upon that cross, I had truly risen far enough in consciousness to understand the true meaning of love and forgiveness. As I ask each of you to simply look deep within yourself and begin to forgive all those who have trespassed against you and all those you have trespassed against. My blessed Mother was the one who taught me about unconditional love and forgiveness. As a family, she would take us into the circle of love and we would simply hold hands, connect deep to Mother Earth and to the four elements and we would simply allow ourselves to release all fear, judgment, pain and sorrow. She taught us if we entered into the circle of love, then the power of the four elements would transform our pain and therein we will be set free. I ask you at this time, if you are feeling judgmental or have a bitter, unforgiving heart, simply allow yourself to enter into the circle of love and bring the power of the four elements into your being. As you learn to ground yourself into the love of Mother Earth, from the top of your head into the soles of your feet, you may truly begin to feel her love as she takes your pain and heals your heart. As you begin to practice holding the power of love from Mother Earth and all of

Great Spirit, you shall begin to you allow yourself to move into the energy of forgiveness. It is truly about letting go and letting God, and allowing your beautiful light to shine. Forgiveness is difficult and many are reluctant to release their burdens, bitterness and pain. But simply allow me to give you my sacred heart of mercy and compassion so that you may have a compassionate heart, a merciful heart and truly feel the love of God.

As you open your compassionate heart to the world, understand all is in divine order. It is simply about allowing, forgiving, letting go and letting God. As you bring the energy of forgiveness through your being, begin to feel the shift within your own consciousness, as you understand there is no need to be afraid or angry. There is only love and there is only allowance. It is by allowing and forgiving that you come back into that state of oneness and the energy of love and peace, in which you were created. As you embody the energy of love and forgiveness, peace and mercy then the memories, the hurt, the pain begin to fade away. Allow God's love and light and peace to enter into your being at its fullest as you hold the essence of the light frequency of *who you truly are*. As you open to the beautiful gifts of love, peace and forgiveness, then and only then, can you begin to embody the gift of joy and love that you bring to this planet. As you hold light within your being and love within your very essence, begin to radiate the energy of love, peace and forgiveness which is so needed upon the planet.

When I walked upon planet Earth 2,000 years ago, my message was indeed about love, forgiveness, acceptance, and allowance. Many did not understand the great design of what was to take place and what I had contracted to do in that lifetime. I chose to be an example of forgiveness and love for the people to learn the principles of the Father. I sacrificed my physical self in order to bring forth the Lesson of Love and forgiveness onto the world. I was fully aware of the great design of what I was to do, fully comprehending that I would be laid on the cross. Not to symbolize that I am the Lord and Savior, for there is nothing to be saved, nor are you sinners. I continue as the Living Christ, to teach the principles and lessons of love and forgiveness for all to embody and embrace into their hearts as physical, spiritual beings on planet Earth. It is unfortunate many continue to hold anger within their hearts regarding my crucifixion, however, this is not necessary for I knew exactly what my mission and the Great Design was to be for my soul's journey. I came simply to teach you, to look beyond the physical and rise up and ascend into higher consciousness, higher teachings, higher understandings. Simply that all is in divine order and all is as it should be. As I have said many times before, I would not want to go through the physical pain again, though it was necessary for my crucifixion to occur and to this day, I hold no anger or judgment against those who had harmed me.

Dearest children, understand it is necessary to release your anger as it does not create justice and balance for anyone, let alone for yourself. Many souls have been persecuted; many have been harmed and injured by another in the name of God. I was one among many who have been sacrificed by the hands of another. I forgave those who harmed me through the power of love and forgiveness. I ask you each to hold the power of love and forgiveness within your system strongly, vibrantly, and powerfully that you will no longer feel the pain. It is indeed a gift of great joy when the releasing of this anger with the energy of forgiveness and allowance come forth as it simply frees you to live your life as you were intended...free to be, free to love and free to serve.

Though this **Lesson of Forgiveness** is an important one, it is so difficult for many people to comprehend and to understand. Many people hold themselves tightly bound to their own emotions, to their own anger, to their own hatred. The concept of forgiveness is difficult for most to understand simply because they feel that the other person has not been held accountable. I simply wish to tell you, my children, that if you hold onto this lower vibration of thinking, you will be the one to suffer, not the other. How many times are you emotionally triggered by a raw emotion that continues to purge from your own physical being? As dear Kryon has said many times, "do you wish to be a part of the problem or do you wish to be a part of the solution?" What do I mean by this? I simply mean that as long as you hold on to your anger and pain, you will remain the victim. I must tell you children, there are no victims or perpetrators, for this is a hard lesson to learn. Simply, understand that all is in divine order and regardless of what you understand about your life, your pain, your sorry, your misery your soul has chosen every experience for you to learn from. You are simply here on this earth plane to learn soul lessons. Your soul knew exactly what you were entering into when you chose to incarnate into your current physical incarnation. The soul's journey is not an easy one. I simply had come before you to help you learn to love, forgive and move forward so that peace may prevail within you and upon planet Earth. It is truly about letting go and letting God for in practicing to be at peace, you shall begin to embody peace. Forgiveness truly frees you and allows you to be in the state of harmony, peace and balance, as you were intended to live here on this Earth plane. When humanity learns to forgive, there will be peace in the hearts of mankind, and peace shall prevail upon Mother Earth.

Dearest children, breathe in the energy of forgiveness within your very essence. Allow me to clear negative energies which have been held within your own memory bank, within your own soul's essence, within your own physical self; so your heart can be open to love. Breathe in the energy of love and the energy of forgiveness as you forgive yourself and forgive those who have harmed you. As you move into a state of peace, balance, harmony, and love; bring the energy of forgiveness within you strongly and fully for in doing so you shall be set free. Let go and let God. Let go and let God. Let go and let God.

For many, these truth teachings may be difficult to understand or even to embrace, but those who are ready will come, those who are ready will listen, and those who are ready will embrace my teachings. As you embrace the lessons of love and forgiveness within your being, you will bring forth the way, light and truth. For love and forgiveness will become all-encompassing as your heart shall open to peace. As you allow this energy to move through your system in its fullest, hold and carry the love and forgiveness in its totality. As you enter into this state of peace, balance, harmony, love, and wholeness you shall live in the freedom and totality of *who you truly are*. In the power of love, there is perfection, wholeness, joy, and freedom. It is simply about freeing yourself from negative emotion, pain, sorrow, and all memories and thoughts that no longer serve you. As you become free of negative emotions, you will draw closer to oneness with the Father and there peace shall enter into your heart. As you master and begin to embody the **Lesson of Forgiveness** do not be afraid to *live in joy and in the remembrance of who you truly are* for in doing so the light and love you hold shall become brighter and stronger with each passing day. Dearest children, know the totality of who you are is truth and the energy you hold carries love so peace and forgiveness can be sent forth onto the world. Understand that which you hold and carry brings forth great power and joy as you live in a state of truth and oneness to all that there is. The power of love *will* bring peace to planet Earth, however, it begins with one person at a time, holding love and peace within their hearts.

As I have spoken earlier about the **Lesson of Oneness**; understand dearest ones, you are sacred spiritual beings. The energy you hold and carry within your thought form, within your body, within your mental and emotional system is sacred. If you are full of hate, bitterness, and anger, then where is the balance? Where is the love? Where is the peace? Where is the balance and harmony in one's life? Remember, dearest children, you are a spark of God; you are co-creators of your own life. Your mind, body and soul are sacred, remember dearest children; you were made in the image of God. You are perfect in the eyes of God.

Dearest children, remember each of you have a responsibility not only to yourself, but to Mother Earth and all of humanity to hold and carry the energy of love within your mind, body, and spirit. This shall bring peace and balance to Mother Earth. Those who misunderstand forgiveness; those who feel it only lets the other person off the hook or absolves them of their wrongful act, will only hurt themselves. As you open your heart to forgive and love someone who has hurt you, this frees you and brings you back into balance. If you wish to be a true peacemaker, if you wish to be a true way shower of my word, of my light; then learn to forgive. As you understand the **Lesson of Forgiveness** it brings peace and balance within your system and for all the world to see.

Dearest children, humanity must return to a balanced and harmonious state in order for peace to prevail upon planet Earth. As you hold peace and love within your being, then you bring the energy of love needed for the balance of Mother Earth. If you hold and carry energies of anger, hatred, and mistrust; then this energy is brought forth to Mother Earth. Many do not understand that Mother Earth is a living, breathing entity and she absorbs your pain, anger and hatred. As you let go and let God and learn to forgive and be at peace you bring balance to yourself and to Mother Earth. The peace and love which you bring to the planet is God's healing energy for we are all one. What affects one, affects another. As you live your life in peace, love and balance you have a enormous opportunity to make a difference, not only in your own life, but in the lives of others and the planet at-large. These truth teachings are for all the masses and are for all who are ready to learn and grow in spiritual consciousness. Do not let yourself be confused with what you do not understand. Dearest children, as you open your heart to these truth teachings and the **Lesson of Forgiveness,** then you may live in a place of balance, peace, and joy. Dearest children, as you understand these lessons, allow the energy of joy to radiate throughout your essence and to the very core of your being.

Dearest children, I wish for you to understand that you each hold and carry the energy of the Christ consciousness within you. I simply want to remind you that you are the current way showers, teachers, and messengers of God's principles and truth teachings; just as I was in my time. Due to modern technology, my teachings can now be brought forth to the masses in a way that was not possible during my ministry 2,000 years ago. I wish for you to understand my ministry and my life continues on; for I am the Living Christ. My life was to be an example of love, peace, allowance, and forgiveness. This is what I ask from each of you: love, allow, forgive and be at peace. Forgive yourself and forgive another and know life is all about love for you are truly living on the planet of love. As you hold and carry this energy of love; radiate it through your vocal cords, your eyes, every cell, every fiber, and every pore of your being. For in doing so, this affects and heals yourself, those who you love, and, yes, those whom you have perceived to have harmed you. Truly forgiveness heals all.

I thank you, dearest children, for your time. I thank you, dearest children, for your attention. I pray all of humanity finds love within their hearts to forgive, to allow, and to let go and let God. As I bring forth the energy of forgiveness and love, this was my message 2,000 years ago and continues to remain my message on this day. As a way shower and messenger of the light, this was my role, to teach humanity how to love, allow, and forgive. I chose to model these truth teachings of love and forgiveness for all to see and I continue my mission today as the Living Christ. My desire is to awaken humanity to these truth teachings in order for peace to prevail upon planet Earth.

Dearest children, go forth in the understanding your life is in balance and all is in divine order. *Live in joy in the remembrance of who you truly are.* You are all one with the Father and all of creation. For humanity must come together in unity for this is what planet Earth longs for. Peace, love and unity will once again return to planet Earth. Mother Earth is the planet of love and she loves each of you deeply, as God loves you. This **Lesson of Forgiveness** is about oneness and no longer living in separation from your fellow brother and sister. It is about bringing forth unity and peace, and the truth, the way, and the light for all the world to see and all the world to know. I thank you, my children. I honor you. I bless you. Go in the understanding that peace and forgiveness shall prevail. And so, it is!

℘ *Lesson of Hope* ℘

Dearest children, it is I Christ. I bring forth **Lesson VII: the Lesson of Hope**. Dearest children, understand this lesson is an opportunity to bring hope onto the world through your actions, thought, deeds, and through your words. As a light worker, you are here to help humanity to evolve into a higher state of consciousness. Hope is an acronym for <u>H</u>elp <u>O</u>ur <u>P</u>eople <u>E</u>volve. All light workers have come at this time to bring love onto the world and to bring hope to this planet and to all of humanity. There are many who will look to each of you for guidance and look to each of you for the truth, the way, and the light. Just as the teachings of Mohammed, Abraham, Krishna, Gandhi, and Buddha brought higher conscious teachings to humanity, each of you are master teachers, and are here to help bring higher conscious teachings to humanity. There are many who will come to you for spiritual guidance and assistance and I ask that you help them understand these truth teachings that I am bringing forth at this time. Humanity's sole purpose is to help this planet evolve into a peaceful and loving planet. Regardless of why you think you are here, all have come forth to help in the evolutionary process of this planet. Even those who do not consciously know of their mission are here to help this planet evolve into a higher state of consciousness. Each soul has chosen to incarnate on this planet to help bring the evolution and ascension of the planet to a higher level of consciousness during this time of the *great ascension.*

Each soul who has incarnated at this time on the planet was a part of the Great Conclave which was spoken about in Dr. Heather Anne Harder's book, <u>Many Were Called, Few Were Chosen</u>. Each soul's mission is truly to bring forth peace, love, and light onto this planet. As I, Christ, spoke at the Great Conclave, there were many spiritual beings of light who volunteered to become the core volunteers to assist planet Earth in its ascension process. If you are reading this book, you are one such volunteer who eagerly chose to incarnate on planet Earth in multiple incarnations in order to assist this planet and all of humanity in order for peace to prevail on planet Earth.

As a core volunteer, your spirit and soul will be drawn to my truth teachings at this time, and as a light-worker, you are indeed responsible for assisting others to understand my truth teachings in order to raise the consciousness of humanity for peace and love to prevail on planet Earth.

The **Lesson of Hope** builds from all the lessons, from all the previous lessons. The **Lesson of Love** is indeed the first lesson because if there is no love, then how can there be hope? As you begin to embrace and embody the Lessons of Love, Power, Truth, Oneness, Enlightenment, and Forgiveness, you shall easily embrace the **Lesson of Hope**. The vibrational energy of hope is indeed quite powerful, because without hope of a better day then fear, anger, lack and loss shall engulf you into separation from God. There are so many souls deceiving themselves by their own ego and mental chatter as they are allowing themselves to be deceived by those in man-made power. Many do not listen to their own still, quiet voice from within, their own intuition and have little faith within them. Many are afraid to trust their own knowingness as many are taught not to listen or trust their own inner guidance. Hope and faith go hand-in-hand, for without faith there is no hope. Dearest children, this **Lesson of Hope** appears to be a challenge for many, but be not afraid to ask God and myself for assistance with your worries and needs. Learn to trust the still, quiet voice within. Quietly learning to let go and let God.

During my ministry over 2,000 years ago, my desire was to bring hope to the people to trust in a higher power and in their own divine power. My message then and my message now remain the same. I came to show humanity a new way of living. My desire was to bring hope and light where there was darkness, fear and loss. My desire as the Living Christ is to instill the energy of hope into all of humanity. The Great I Am has imprinted the energy of hope into the soul's essence of all beings as God has gifted each of you with hope as your birthright. There are many celestial beings of light, all of your star brothers and sisters, all who have come from different planetary and galactic forms have come to help assist this planet and humanity to bring hope to the world. When I walked upon this earth plane 2,000 years ago, my desire was to awaken all who would listen in order to open their hearts to feel the energy of peace, love and hope for all the world to see and to know. As you read these words, my desire is for you to connect to a deeper sense of *who you truly are*, knowing that your birthright is indeed hope. There will be many who will be drawn to you, like a moth to a flame, who have lost their way and are in need hope and faith in order to spiritually awaken. It is your responsibility as a light-worker to take the hand of another...*for each one teach one, each one lead one.* As you help another soul connect to their own innate wisdom, there you help yourself as you feel the presence of the divine moving so powerfully, so purely within your own being. Please help your fellow brother and sister to understand that the energy of hope has been ingrained within their being as their birthright. God has gifted you with hope to carry on during times of strife and struggle. There are so many souls who are lost, who need direction, understanding, love and peach and truly need a sense of hope in their troubled lives. When you look at your own inner stirrings, as you look into your own inner callings, is there not hope for your future? Is there not hope for your dreams? Is there not hope you will continue to evolve and grow closer to the Father? Or do you remain in a place of sadness, loneliness, anger, and fear? Do you feel confused, disconnected, and separated from yourself and God? It is time to understand the energy of hope is ingrained within you and is genetically a part of your birthright. God's gift to you is your inner knowingness. There are many who have lost connection to their own innate wisdom and have lost connection to the essence of *who they truly are* as many have forgotten to *live in joy and remembrance of who they truly are.* And yet, there are many who hold onto the belief of hope as the last straw. H.O.P.E. is about helping people awaken to the new age of enlightenment which is truly the energy of the divine feminine. The energy of the divine feminine is the energy of love, peace, compassion and mercy for all of humanity. This is the energy being brought forth at this time. This is the energy that will bring peace to all, for as we hold faith and hope within our hearts, we shall build on the principles of God's teachings for peace to prevail.

Dearest children of the light, you are all collectively connected to this book, <u>The Twelve Mastery Teachings of Christ</u>. Each of you hold and carry the vibration of the Christ essence within as you read this book. It is my desire that you begin to embody all the teachings and embrace them with a loving and open and hopeful heart. Hold and carry the vibration of hope as you hold and carry the other eleven truth teachings. Dearest children, it is a lesson of great consequence as you enter into a place of peace and love inside of you, as you bring hope to the world. Never underestimate these truth teachings, never underestimate the power of love you hold and carry within your hearts, and never underestimate the light you bring, which is indeed love. Go forth in your knowingness. Go forth in your strength. Go forth in your light and go forth in hope.

Dearest children, when I brought the **Lesson of Hope** to the people 2,000 years ago, many listened, yet many turned away from my truth teachings. As a way shower and messenger, you are to help others understand what they hold and carry within them is the law of attraction, like attracts like. However, be prepared for others not to understand you as your vibrational frequency may be incompatible to those you are ministering to. So many do not understand that their thoughts are energy so become aware of the power of your thoughts for you are a co-creator with God.

The lesson of hope is necessary at this time, not only for the survival of the planet, but for the survival of all of humanity. There are many souls who came to planet Earth to help bring peace to this planet. If you are reading this book then you are one of the light workers who is helping the planet evolve as a loving and peaceful planet. Many such magnificent beings of light were Martin Luther King, Mother Theresa, Princess Diana and Gandhi, to name a few. These beings sacrificed themselves in order to bring a higher level of conscious teachings to the people. They chose to sacrifice themselves in order to bring peace, love, light, and hope to this planet. It is the energy of peace and love which allows the planet to thrive. There are many loving energies flooding planet Earth at this time to help awaken humanity to higher conscious teachings.

There are many who misunderstand the meaning of the age of enlightenment or the new age movement, as it is about bringing peace, love and unity to all of humanity and to all of creation. For this movement represents the energy of the divine feminine in its fullest. Peace, love, compassion and mercy for humanity are the prevailing energy of the new age of enlightenment. It is bringing change and hope to many beings as so many have lived in fear of change. Many are frightened of moving forward into change, but change is a natural cycle of life and should not be feared. In 2012, Mother Earth has now ascended into the energy of peace, hope, love and unity and now humanity must catch up in their own individual ascension process. The time of the great awakening has now arrived as humanity must return to a balanced and harmonious state in order for peace to prevail upon planet Earth.

Dearest children, entering into the totality of *who you truly are* is about embodying the energy of peace, hope and love. The energy of hope is held as a vibrational light frequency within each of you. Look within and hold this energy within your heart and never give up hope. Never allow yourself to succumb to the fear which is brought primarily through the media to the masses. Remember to stay focused on your soul's mission, as you shall have courage to remain in your true divine power to complete your life's purpose. Each of my <u>Twelve Mastery Teachings</u> have a powerful healing vibration within each lesson as they hold and carry the power of God's healing energy in it truest essence. These twelve mastery teachings are aligned to the peace and unity grid that Kryon has built around Mother Earth in 2001. Mother Earth has been aligned to my truth teachings at her very heart and core, however, as Kryon has built the peace and light grid around the planet, she is beginning to feel greater power and the true essence of these energies in her fullest form. As peace and unity are now prevailing upon planet Earth, many are feeling these energies, as well. Do not let the energies upon the planet frighten you, but embrace these energies as they were offered in love. The past and present earth changes have represented the realignment of Mother Earth's energy so that peace and love can prevail on our beautiful planet.

Dearest children, the energy of hope is the vibrational frequency that is closest to humanity. The other vibrations have their own frequencies, but this particular lesson, this particular teaching, is closest to the consciousness of humanity. As you hold the essence of hope closely to your heart and heart chakra, allow the energy of compassion, mercy, and love to resonate throughout your being. Dearest ones, as you enter into this new state of being, carry the energy of hope, peace, and love for all to feel. Understand this energy is potent and powerful, as it is the energy of God. Just as you have been gifted with your own intuition and God has granted you many gifts, you have been innately given the gift of hope to keep moving forward into this journey called life. If you are experiencing many life struggles/challenges, understand that they are simply life and soul lessons. As a light worker you have chosen to enter into your life incarnation to learn many earthly lessons, therefore, hold and carry the banner of hope to move forward in knowing there is a brighter day. Yes, it is my teachings that shall help you to embody strength and fortitude coupled with faith to carry on that life was not meant to be filled with strife or struggle, but simply to be enjoyed.

Dearest children, as I teach these principles and help people understand life is a journey and all is in divine order, the energy of hope is a gift from God. The **Lesson of Hope** is one of the most important in all of the Twelve Mastery Truth teachings. The **Lesson of Hope** was given to you so you can carry on regardless of the strife and struggles you have on your earth plane. We have not left humanity without the tools, the guidance, and the assistance of the angelic realm; including the archangels, the celestial beings, I, my mother, and all who have come forth to assist humanity. When you are embody my truth teachings you are connected to love. Dearest children of the light, hold these principles closely to your essence. Allow yourself to radiate the energy of hope, as it moves through you, know you are a true child of the light, fully embodied with love and fully embodied with the energy of hope.

I thank you, dearest children for your time and your attention. I ask you to bring hope onto the world, as it is so needed. This **Lesson of Hope** is given from the Father to assist in awakening humanity to their own divinity. HOPE (Help Our People Evolve) and bring this planet and humanity back to the state of oneness and the state of perfection it was meant to be. Go in peace. Go in light. Go in love.

And so, it is!

‭ஐ *Lesson of Faith* ‭ය

Dearest children, it is I, Christ. I bring forth **Lesson VIII: The Lesson of Faith**. Understand, dearest children, there are many levels of faith that are brought forward into this journey called life. The light you hold within your system is composed of several rays of light. One of the energies you hold and carry within each of you is the divine energy of faith. The vibrational frequency of faith is truly a gift from the heavens. Just as the **Lesson of Faith** carries its own vibration, the energies of love, power, truth, oneness, enlightenment, forgiveness, and hope hold their own vibrational frequencies as well.

As you enter into a state of oneness, you are brought closer to the truth of *who you truly are*. With each breath you take, you hold and carry the energy of faith and it shall manifest even deeper within your soul's essence. Those who hold and carry the frequency of faith will bring forth this energy onto the world. It is not that you can acquire faith through what you call osmosis, but it is a development within the soul that deepens within the being who remains connected to divine source.

Many on your planet have lost their connection to faith as many have lost their connection to divine truth. There are countless lost souls walking around this planet without love, peace and faith within their hearts. So many souls are living without purpose within their own lives. Some are confused about what they are to do with themselves and what they are to do with their life purpose and their life path. They move from relationship to relationship and job to job in hopes of seeking peace within their souls as they truly are seeking their own soul's expression.

Without insight into their own spiritual connection, these souls have lost hope and have lost their connection to the divine. Many are searching to find the truth, the way, and the light within them as they yet many are looking to find peace and comfort in all the wrong places. Searching externally and looking outward to be told what to think, to be told what to do, and yet, it is about turning inward and connecting to the divine source. Dearest children of the light, the hope you carry, the light you carry, and the joy you carry within your system is truly about embracing faith and love within your own heart. The power of faith is the key to bringing forth the law of attraction within your own life and within the world around you. Hope and faith go hand in hand in order to manifest and create your life as you are co-creators with the divine.

Do not be surprised by the changes you see within yourself and within the world around you as you begin to deepen your faith to the divine. As you connect to the divine, you will have greater peace within your heart. The new energy frequencies upon the planet are awakening individuals at a rapid rate as there are many more who are looking to be brought closer to God's light. During my time on Earth, over 2,000 years ago, there were many who were frightened and lost and looking to develop their connection to the divine. It is the same today as many souls are searching to understand their life path and divine purpose. Many wish to project their anger and blame onto God. Many have become lost and desolate due to challenges and lessons of the soul. As you begin to allow the energy of faith to awaken within, the energy of my light and the light of the Father will truly allow you to deepen your connection to the divine. All is in divine order and all is as it should be. Without faith, there is no hope, and without hope, there is no faith.

Dearest children, truly begin to understand that all is in divine order and all is as it should be because there is a reason for all that occurs, regardless of whether you understand on a conscious level. For this is the lesson of faith and hope as one begins to develop a spiritual understanding that tragedies in one's life truly are have a higher purpose. Life is in a constant state of change, nothing was ever meant to remain the same. This is where faith and hope come in as fear can be quite paralyzing and devastating to one's soul without a spiritual understanding that all is at it should be and all is in divine order. For those who choose to remain angry, fearful, depressed, lonely, my message for you today is simply to let go and to let God. The **Lesson of Faith** is truly a powerful one as it is the key to unlocking the door to a new understanding that we are all one and that we are all connected. What you choose to do with your own emotions is simply your own choice, but if you choose to live a life of spiritual freedom, allow yourself to expand your consciousness to a higher perspective.

As you allow yourself to feel the connection of the energy of the divine, allow the energy of faith to deepen within you, as you hold and carry it close to your heart. It is by embodying the energy of faith that will help you through life's challenges. As you grow in the essence of love, power, truth, oneness, enlightenment, forgiveness, hope, and faith you will feel the peace within you even stronger. All is as it should be. There are no accidents for every event is orchestrated for the higher purpose for all concerned. As you begin to embrace this understanding and deepen your faith, this is when you truly can let go and let God, awakening to the essence of *who you truly are.*

Dearest children, as you hold and carry the energy of faith, it becomes infectious. It is not something you can acquire, it is to be embodied for it truly is a sense of knowingness held deep within you. The energy of faith is knowingness. As you grow stronger in faith with each passing day, know your life is in divine order. Never underestimate the power of *who you truly are.* The love you hold deep within your essence is light, joy, and peace. Listen to your internal ticking and listen to your own intuition. Listen to your own heart and listen to my message of love. Dearest children, God enfolds each soul with His energy of love and faith. And yet, regardless of what you think, of what you feel, this is your divine gift from God as it is your birthright. I, Christ, am here to help you understand that the vibrational frequencies of all the lessons have been imprinted into your soul's essence by God. I've come to help to awaken all souls who have chosen to close themselves off from God's gifts of grace. It is time to open your hearts to love. Allow the light you hold, the love you hold, and the peace you hold to bring forth the essence of faith onto the world. I, Christ, wish to bring forth these teachings to help all reconnect to their own innate wisdom, knowingness, and truth. Dearest children, embrace these vibrational frequencies in order for others to feel the energy of love and faith radiating from your being.

The **Lesson of Faith** is simplistic, yet powerful. In its simplicity, the power of faith is the power of God. It is the Holy Spirit that works through your being. The richness and fullness you hold and carry within your essence is the vibrational frequency of God. As you allow faith to deepen within your heart, your burdens and worries will begin to diminish. Life will then become easier, as you begin to radiate joy and peace through holding faith in your heart. As you move through your world with speed, you miss the opportunity to allow yourself to unfold, blossom and become the beautiful being you are. Allow yourself to accept your own divine power, step into the energy and vibrational frequency of faith. Allow faith to be your compass on this journey called life. Claim the vibrational frequency of faith which is your innate connection to God for God has not forsaken you. He has given you these teachings in order to assist you in your soul's journey with greater ease. Open your compassionate and merciful heart to the world, for there will be many who will doubt, question and challenge you about my teachings. As you truly develop your own understanding of the divine, you will be able to become a messenger and teacher, embodying faith within your essence. Therefore, allow your faith to deepen, and know the truth within your essence is the energy of God. Dearest children, as you allow yourself to grow stronger within the truth of who you are, know love is all that there is for the energy of the Father is always with you. Never doubt yourself. Hold strong to your faith in God.

As you embrace faith in its fullest, there and then can you live your life in freedom and in the oneness of *who you truly are*. Know and understand the truth, the way, and the light within you is love. When you lack faith, your connection to God becomes weakened with fear and stagnant energy and then separation from God occurs. As you realign your energy to God, allow the vibrational frequency of faith to enter into your being so that you may feel whole and complete in oneness to the Father. Dearest children, as you understand these teachings, go forth in your daily life and share these teachings with the world. Through prayer and meditation, the energy of faith will grow stronger. Faith is important, for without faith, there can be no hope and without hope there is no faith. All the Twelve Mastery Teachings build upon one another so simply allow yourself to spiritually grow at your own pace.

My children, go with the knowledge that this connection within each of you must be nurtured for faith cannot be acquired, it can only be nurtured. As you allow the energy of faith to move through you, allow it to grow stronger within your physical being and within the essence of *who you truly are*. I thank you, dearest children, for your time, attention, love, and devotion. I thank you for allowing this vibrational frequency of faith to grow stronger with the essence of *who you truly are.* As you grow stronger in your connection to God, your faith will deepen with each passing day. Faith is God's gift of grace, and a beloved one, at that. Go in love, go in light, and go in peace. Go forth in the strength of your own faith. I thank you. I love you. I honor you.

And so, it is!

ઠ Lesson of Rejuvenation ભ

Dearest children, it is I, Christ. I bring forth **Lesson IX, The Lesson of Rejuvenation**. It is about rejuvenating the soul, living in joy and remembrance of *who you truly are*. God has granted you the gift of life and your life is to be used for divine purpose and good. As you awaken each morning to this gift of life, allow your body, mind, and soul to be rejuvenated with the gift of love and rejuvenation from the Father. Each day is a gift from God. Each day is an opportunity to bring forth the gifts God has brought onto you.

The energy of rejuvenation is the vital life force within you for it truly is the energy of God. Many may call this chi, prana or the holy spirit. The energy of rejuvenation is truly expressed through children as you see their love, joy, freedom, vitality and innocence expressed in their being. Know dearest children, the love, joy, freedom and innocence a child holds is also within you, for it is your birthright. God is gifting you with the energy of rejuvenation as it will rejuvenate the mind, body and spirit. So many people are searching for the fountain of youth. What they are truly searching for is the energy of rejuvenation, the vital life force of God. You too, can embrace and embody the fountain of youth, for it is your God-given right. As you spend time in quiet meditation, call forth the energy of rejuvenation to bring you perfect peace, health and happiness within your being. Never underestimate this power of rejuvenation for it will help you to live in freedom and remembrance of *who you truly are*. Dearest children, never underestimate the power you bring forth onto this world. Allow the rejuvenation of your body, mind and soul to come forth for this will bring peace onto you. When you begin to realize that you can regenerate and rejuvenate your body and mind as an eternal spirit, then there will be no fear of growing old. Simply allow peace to be your birthright. Allow the Father to bring peace within your own soul and within your own soul's essence as you begin to embody and embrace the energy of rejuvenation.

The gift of rejuvenation is a gift from God. This gift of rejuvenation does not have to be sought after or searched for. It is already within you, just call upon the wellspring of God's vital life force. All you have to do is ask and allow God to bring the energy of rejuvenation upon you. So many souls searching for a youth potion. What you have forgotten is the potion is not outside of yourself, but within you. It is the energy, the wellspring, of rejuvenation that is within you. You are a divine being. You are a spark of God. Therefore, that spark, that rejuvenation of the vital life force of God is within you. All you have to do is ask for it each and every day. All you have to do is call upon this energy and you are rejuvenated. Simply go into the temple of rejuvenation each and every night and ask to be rejuvenated in your mind, body and spirit. Simply allow all that no longer serves you to be released.

Dearest children, do not be afraid of living and do not be afraid of dying. Look upon each day as a gift and do not be afraid of the next day or what is around the corner. Live each day to the fullest. Do not be afraid to give and do not be afraid to love. And certainly, do not be afraid to bring forth the wellspring, the rejuvenation of life from God into your being. The gift God has given you is life. Simply make a choice each and every day to live your life in the fullest as you make the choice to live from your true soul and spirit essence. Give freely of the gifts of your soul for what you give to the world, you shall receive for yourself. Your special gifts, your special talents, perhaps a smile, a kindness, a warm pat on the back, whatever you have to give, whatever you have to offer, this will rejuvenate you. As you give you shall receive. In so going, this will allow the wellspring of the Father's energy to rejuvenate within you each and every day. God's vital life force is eternal. Remember, the energy of rejuvenation is always there to call upon. It is yours. It is yours. It is yours. Do not be afraid to love. Do not be afraid to love. Do not be afraid to love. Live and let live. Live and let live. Live and let live. Do not be afraid to be the expression of divine love as this love is truly the vitality and innocence of the divine child within.

In my time, 2,000 years ago, the energy of rejuvenation was given to me in a dream. The energy of the life force began to spring up within me. Just as a geyser, that energy began to emerge within me on my 25th year. There I began to feel the energy of the Father within me ever so deeply, ever so fully, ever so powerfully. I began to feel the energy with every breath, with every step I took. It rejuvenated me. It motivated me. It was my life and continues to be. The energy of the Father is within me, as it is within you. I am no different than you. I understand your struggles and human emotions. For I too, had doubts about my own divine mission. My <u>Twelve Mastery Teachings</u> are the teachings from the Father. I struggled with bringing them to the masses over 2,000 years ago and now I am returning to bring the essence of my teachings once again. These teachings are to be used in a very sacred manner as they are *not just for a select group, but these teachings are universal.* They are to be used for humanity to understand the power of God that is within each soul. These teachings are your God-given right. They are from the Father and from the Mother and are from the energy of Great Central Sun.

Dearest children as I stated during my time on Earth as Jesus of Nazareth, I struggled with bringing forth God's messages onto the world. Many did listen, yet, many turned their heads away. When I became tired and weak during my ministry, I would go to the waters of the Sea of Galilee and allow the wellspring of the energy of rejuvenation to heal my tired mind, body and soul. The mere act of allowing myself time to rest and rejuvenate thus allowed me to continue on with my ministry. The time has come again for the energy of rejuvenation to be brought forth onto this planet in a new way, on a grander scale. I wish for humanity to access the energy of rejuvenation as these current times are, indeed, stressful and many are losing their connection to themselves, including their connection to the divine. As you live your life disconnected from the energy of oneness, this is how you begin to weaken and age. For those who may not understand, you can truly rejuvenate yourself by simply using your intention and entering into the temple of rejuvenation during your quiet, meditative time. I Christ, bring these <u>Twelve Mastery Teachings</u> forth for humanity to embrace and embody in their fullest essence. I wish for you to understand all of these teachings, all of these principles are your God-given right. The energy of rejuvenation is the vital life force within you, the energy of *who you truly are.* This is the energy of the totality of all you are. This is the energy of love, peace, and joy.

Dearest children, never underestimate the power of what you bring forth. You are a child of the light and a child of love. The energy of rejuvenation is truly within you and is your birthright. The energy of rejuvenation is within you. You are free to love. You are free to be. You are free to serve. I do not wish to belabor the point, but it is important for you to understand you are a wellspring, and the energy of God is within you. Many have forgotten this as many have lost their connection to God. The energy of rejuvenation is truly the eternal fountain of youth you are all looking for. It will not be found in a bottle or a cream. There is no need to chop up your bodies to find beauty. There is no need to try to recreate and make something you are not. You are already perfect just the way you are. Eternal youth comes from within. As it radiates from within, you become radiant, you are beautiful. You are whole. You are complete. You are beautiful. You are loved.

As you begin to accept yourself, know God is within. When you begin to feel the wellspring of God within you, then you are truly radiant and you are truly beautiful. There is no need to change, no need to hate yourself, for in doing so you are dishonoring the temple that is God. There is no need to dishonor yourself, no need to criticize yourself, for you were created in the image of God. *Serenity Prayer:* "God grant me the serenity to accept the things I cannot change; courage to change the things I can; and wisdom to know the difference."

As you accept yourself, you are able to love yourself unconditionally and in doing so, you are then able to love others unconditionally. Do not underestimate the power of *who you truly are*, for remember dearest children that you were created in the image of God. You are God. Live in the essence of *who you truly are*. Live in the freedom of who you are. Live in the joy of who you are. Live in the light of *who you truly are*. You are free. You are free. You are free. Do not be afraid to love. Do not be afraid to give. Do not be afraid to express yourself in the fullest. Never underestimate the power of who you truly are, for you are love and you are light. This energy of rejuvenation is the life force within you that allows you to create and recreate yourself. This energy of rejuvenation is the spark of God. It is the creation of new life. Some say it is a miracle. Yes, it is a miracle, a miracle from God. Rejuvenate yourself and love yourself. Allow the energy of God to enter into your being and know the truth of *who you truly are*, the peace of who you truly are, and the love of who you truly are. Begin to radiate the energy of rejuvenation and then you will find the fountain of youth you have been searching for. Then the radiance of God may shine through your face, eyes and within your physical system. Dearest children, know each soul is a spark of light, and allow God's light to grow within you, for this is your God-given right.

Allow yourself to be free. Allow yourself to love, and above all, love yourself. The energy of rejuvenation is a powerful, potent energy for it is that which created you and that which created the world. As you begin to look within, you are rejuvenated with the energy of God. Live and let live. Live and let live. Live and let live. Allow yourself to go in the peace and the joy and the *remembrance of who you truly are*. You are God. You are God. You are God.

And so, it is!

ஓ Lesson of Remembrance ෬

Dearest children, it is I, Christ. I bring forth **Lesson X, the Lesson of Remembrance**. This **Lesson of Remembrance** is a grand lesson as it truly connects you to the divine. Allow yourself to be restored in this energy of remembrance. Allow yourself to be restored in peace and love, as you hold the energy of remembrance within your essence so fully and so richly.

Dearest children, as each of you were sparked and created in the image of the Father; you hold the likeness and the image of His light and His love. God's light is brought forth in your soul's essence and physical being. It is held within every cell, every fiber, and every pore of your being thus allowing you to be rejuvenated, awakened, and activated with the new energy frequencies that are now present on the Earth plane at this time. As you bring forth the light within your system, you hold and carry the vibration of the Father within you. It is necessary for each of you to hold this vibration within your system in its purest form at all times. This is the gift of the day, to activate God's light even further within your system. Your physical body can hold a certain degree of divine light by your mere presence, but it is the energy of remembrance which awakens God's light within you even greater. As you hold God's light within, understand your presence can be blinding to those who are not compatible to your level of light frequency. As you increase your light frequency, you may not be energetically compatible with those around you, therefore, be not afraid of letting go of people, places or things that no longer serve you.

Dearest children, it is important you hold and carry God's light within your system. Your bodies were and are designed to hold God's light to a mere 55% of the Father's energy. Most beings do not hold the energy of light within their system even at what you call 1%. God's light within is your birthright, as it was given to you as a gift from the Father. As you hold God's light within your consciousness, sub consciousness, physical body, etheric & auric fields, and within your soul and spirit essence you shall radiate God's healing light upon this planet. The energy of remembrance simply is a reminder to consciously hold God's light as a tribute and an honor to the Father and also a tribute and honor to yourself. Those around you will feel this shifting and changing within your vibrational frequency as you allow this gift of remembrance to awaken you to *who you truly are. Live in joy and remembrance of who you truly are.*

As I, Christ activate the energy of remembrance within you, please place your feet firmly upon the ground and allow the energy to come from your crown chakra, aligning your entire chakra system and into the Earth star chakra. As you bridge this energy between heaven and earth, you are a physical conduit of God's love and light, as above, so below. This lesson of remembrance is a reminder that you are a spiritual being living on Earth. As your physical body is a conduit of light for Mother Earth and all of humanity, you are truly the expression of truth, love and light. Those who stand in your presence shall feel God's love and light within your presence. Again, remember dearest children, not all will be compatible to your light frequency for they are not able to resonate with the high percentage of light you carry at this time. This does not mean that you are to place yourself above another, but simply everything is energy and like attracts like. This is the law of attraction and it is one of the universal laws. Everything has an energy frequency and a vibration and as you grow into the higher frequencies of God's love and light, you are becoming lighter and lighter and rising higher into the ascension process. I ask each of you to raise your vibrational frequency by allowing God's light to enter within your system even further then you can imagine. Those who carry this energy within them, those who acknowledge this energy within them, those who allow this energy to work through their systems shall be in perfect health, vibrancy, joy, peace, love, balance, and harmony. The light of the Father is indeed love. This is the energy of God's creation which is love. As you bring in the energy of remembrance, allow this to be the focus and remembrance of *who you truly are.*

Dearest children, there are seven rays of light that are frequencies of light which can help accelerate one's spiritual growth. These rays encompass the causal body of man, and each ray holds various spiritual and physical qualities. The seven rays of light represent each and every vibration in nature, space and form, and they permeate all objects, all beings and all events in manifestation. Specific qualities of the seven rays of light are connected to the seven chakras. All of these light frequencies are held within your system at a rate that you are able to embody, The capacity to hold and carry the energy of each ray or multiple rays depends upon one's own vibrational frequency. All souls hold and carry the seven rays within their causal body, yet there are pre-dominate rays specific to your energetic fields. Many know this as the colors of your auric field which can change depending on your mood, attitude, physical, mental and emotional health. Understand, dearest children, many beings are able to read the auric field or sense the rays of light surrounding your physical body. As you align yourself to these rays of light, you are holding and carrying the remembrance of the power of God within you. Each spiritual ray changes as you spiritually grow and evolve.

Dearest children, the light of God shines upon you as blue, yellow, pink, white, green, ruby and violet rays of light. Each ray is powerful in its own right and carries its own spiritual attributes. The blue ray is the first ray of light and represents the power of intent, cause, direction, centralization, unity, and divine will. The yellow ray is the second ray of light and is the ray of divine consciousness. This is a ray of wisdom, sensitivity, intuition, and enlightenment. The third ray is a pink light of divine love, tolerance, adoration and gentleness. The fourth ray of white light stands in the middle of the seven rays, and as such it symbolizes a central point of balance and harmony. It stimulates creativity, art and beauty. The white ray represents purification and the ascension process. The green ray of light is the flame of balance, truth and discernment. It leads to analysis and development of ideas, especially divine ideas which produces wisdom and light. The sixth ray is ruby and is a ray of love, devoted service, spiritual healing and idealism. The basic attribute is the quality of peace, understanding, and acceptance of divine truth. The seventh ray is violet and is the most tangible and most expressive of all seven light rays in the visible world. It reflects the quality and relationship that exist between spirit and matter, and due to these properties, is sometimes called ceremonial or magical...a ray of rhythm, ritual, divine law and order, organization and group consciousness. It carries along the divine qualities of love, mercy, compassion, spiritual transfiguration and transformation, along with freedom. St. Germaine is associated with the violet flame of transmutation.

As you hold these rays of light within your energy field and fully within your essence, you begin to understand the importance and the power of these rays of light within your system. The density of energy you may feel in others, the density of energy you may feel within yourself, is the absence of light in its fullest. As you raise your light frequency you shall hold even greater frequencies of light within you. Dearest children, at the time of your physical transition, you will ascend based on the level of spiritual awakening (spiritual light) you hold within your system.

My dearest children know that the essence of your light frequency is peace, love and light. Honor your physical temple and honor your spiritual self, as pure love and pure light. Your light is the connection to the joy and remembrance of *who you truly are*. The light you hold within your system is about honor and reverence to the God and Goddess, and to the divinity you hold within. Those around you will feel a change within you as you allow your frequencies and vibrational rates to increase to the even greater level of God's light and love.

Dearest children, the energy of remembrance is your birthright and you are awakening to it as I speak. As you allow these energies to integrate within your being, I wish to help you to understand these truth teachings are for all to receive and to understand. These teachings are designed to raise the vibrations of humanity, to increase the light frequency upon this planet and to assist Mother Earth in her own ascension process.

Dearest children, understand the peace you hold, the light you hold, and the energy you carry is your birthright of remembrance. It is the energy of remembrance that aligns you to the energy of the Father in its fullest. In your conscious awareness, hold the energy of remembrance within you for God's light and love is *who you truly are*. This light is the totality of all that is and all you shall become. *Live in the joy and remembrance of who you truly are.*

Dearest children, I infuse each of you with the seven rays of light within each of your beings. As you hold and carry the rays of light, understand these frequencies will begin to manifest within each of you and you shall grow closer to the true essence of your divine self.. Go in peace. Go in light. Go in love.

And so, it is!

✌ *Lesson of Peace* ☙

Dearest children, it is I, Christ. I bring forth **Lesson XI: The Lesson of Peace.** World peace is here and peace on earth is now prevailing on planet Earth. Regardless of what you feel and what you see in your world around you, world peace is now here. How can that be you say? Dearest children, understand that the energy of peace is now spreading around the globe like wildfire. Due to the increase of the enlightenment process of many souls, unity and peace is now reigns upon the planet. It begins with one person at a time, simply allow peace to embody your own being and you shall become a peacemaker and bring world peace around the globe. Do not focus on the chaos, violence, negativity, dissension, and fear upon your planet. Instead, realize that as you begin to live and embody peace, this is how peace shall begin to prevail on planet Earth. Each one teach one, each one lead one. For truly there is much peace, light and love upon the planet.

Remember, dearest children, you are the truth, the way, and the light. You are the peacemakers and the peacekeepers for this planet. All of you who have chosen to be in service are peacekeepers to this planet. Those of you who have chosen to be the new way showers and to be the peacekeepers for the planet have chosen the path of ascension, peace and divine power. It is peace that God has given you as your birthright, just as the other ten lessons have been given as your birthright for this divine power is generated from within.

This lesson of peace is the gateway, the star gate, and the energy of the ascension process. The number 11 is the energy of peace. This is why I've chosen peace to be the eleventh lesson of my teachings. You see this number as the powerful numerological symbol, many call it 11:11, as it is the gateway to ascension, simply said this powerful number symbolizes peace. So, whenever you see the number 11, it energetically shall bring you peace. Those who have the number 11 within their birth year are peacekeepers. Now that the year of 2012 has come and gone, the enlightenment process is bringing peace more powerfully on the planet at this time for there are many now who are teaching God's principles and are bringing peace, love, unity and harmony to the planet as we speak.

Dearest children, the light you bring to this planet is the power of God's peace. It is the energy of love, power, truth, oneness, enlightenment, forgiveness, hope, faith, rejuvenation, remembrance, peace and joy. Those who stand in the light and stand in the energy of peace will bring forth truth within their own beings. God has given you the gift of innate wisdom to tap into your own divine truth and power. Simply open the palms of your hands to receive peace and bring this beautiful energy within your being in its fullest. If you choose to be a peacemaker and bring peace to the world, call upon the energy of peace to enter into your system, and call upon this energy to be brought forth within your home, your workplace, within your community and around the globe.

The new Messiah has been born and within a few years this Messiah will be revealed onto the world. After the great shift of consciousness and clearing upon your planet, the new Messiah will be revealed when the planet is ready for the new Messiah. As humanity raises its consciousness, then peace will come forth even greater on planet Earth. We are now in the last 10,000 year cycle for the evolutionary process for Mother Earth for peace to prevail upon planet Earth. For we have now shifted into the new age of enlightenment and peace can fully be actualized and Mother Earth can return back to the planet of peace and love as she was created.

The new age of enlightenment is solely the energy of the divine feminine which is peace, compassion, mercy and love. Allow yourself to awaken to the energy of the divine feminine and begin to embrace and embody the energy of peace and love. Remember to embrace the energy of peace within as it is your birthright for it is the energy in which you were created. As in the last lesson of remembrance, you shall emanate your radiant light of peace and love onto the world as you *live in joy and remembrance of who you truly are.*

Dearest children, what is happening upon the planet with the earth changes is simply a clearing, shifting, and releasing of old energies that no longer serve this new age of enlightenment. Do not fear what you do not understand about what is occurring upon your planet. It will be revealed to the masses within the next few years. Once the new Messiah has been brought forth, the higher vibrational frequencies on the planet will triumph over the fear, violence, chaos and destructive energies. At this time, all beings will have the opportunity to embody the love, peace, compassion, and mercy within their hearts. Currently, your planet is held firmly in the changing, shifting, and transformational energies from the old patriarchal rule to the new divine feminine. Mother Earth must shift and change her vibrational frequencies to be able to hold peace and love within her being. As you embrace peace within yourself, honor the transformational process towards peace, which is occurring upon your planet. There is no need to be afraid of Mother Earth or of what you call your earth changes. It is all a part of the transformation into the energy of the divine feminine. There is no need to be afraid of change, for all is in divine order. As you stay aligned in your mission, as you stay aligned in your purpose, as you stay aligned in the divine order of all there is; open your heart to begin to make those changes and transformations in your own life that brings peace to the world. Those who are peacekeepers and way showers will understand and honor what I am trying to teach.

The new children arriving on this planet are highly evolved spiritual beings who are bringing peace, love and light to planet Earth. These special children have a powerful mission...to bring peace and love to this planet. The special children arrive fully spiritually awakened and knowing who they truly are. More and more of these children are choosing to incarnate on planet Earth to help with the ascension process and assist their elders in their own spiritual awakening. If you are reading this, you are one of the pioneers who have also chosen to enlighten humanity in order for the new children to begin to bring in the age of enlightenment. Simply put, all the light workers are here to hold the energy and to hold the space of love for the new generation of children who will bring peace and unity onto planet Earth. It is not an easy task or an easy mission; however, it is one that each of you has agreed to bring forth out of love for Mother Earth and all of creation.

Dearest children, understand the light frequency you hold is of peace, love, and the energy of transformation. This transformational time in your lives and in the evolution of the planet depends on each of you to hold and carry the energy of peace. Each of you are to be the peacemakers and to bridge the energy between the old patriarchal society and as we move into the energy of the divine feminine (the age of enlightenment). Each of you are the truth, the way, and the light of all that there is. You are the messengers and teachers awakening mankind to my <u>Twelve Mastery Teachings</u>. As I walked upon this planet over 2,000 years ago, my mission was simply about love, forgiveness and peace. As the living Christ, I am again bringing forth the energy of peace to each of you through the essence of my teachings. My gift to you today is a gift for each of you to have the strength and the courage to share and bring forth my teachings onto the masses. As you reclaim your birthright as a physical spiritual being, begin to embody and hold God's light and love within your being. All you have to do is reclaim it, embody it, and be still and know that you are God.

Dearest children, do not allow yourself to be caught up in what you do not understand about your own life or the meaning of your existence. Do not allow yourself to be caught up in world affairs, what you understand to be a declining economy, a fear-based world or a war- based mentality of the people on your planet. The energy of peace is lifting and clearing the destructive and negative energies as I speak. This planet is the planet of love and all is in divine order. There are many beings that are working for peace on behalf of this planet and make the choice to be a peacekeeper and a way shower of my light, my love and my peace. If you choose to be a peacekeeper then truly embody the energy of peace and love within your being for it is in surrendering, allowing and trusting that allows you to truly connect to the divine. Let go and let God. Allow yourself to surrender, to trust, and allow; knowing truth will prevail upon this planet. Do not allow yourself to become involved in hatred, violence, warring, or negativity. Yes, there are dualities and they do exist. Each person has free will choice. Each person has the energy within them to make a difference and a change upon this planet. You can become a part of the problem or you can become a part of the solution. It is your choice. It is, indeed, your free will choice. What will you choose? Peace or fear?

Dearest children, I want you to understand the energy of the Christ, the Christ Consciousness within you is the *second coming of Christ*. No, I will not make my second coming as an appearance in the skies. This may be a surprise to many that I will not appear again in physical form. However, I am bringing my energy to you through these truth teachings. My energy is already present. It is already here for all of you. Many call to me in prayer waiting for me to do their own inner work and to bring them a miracle. Many are waiting for me to show them a sign that I am here. Dearest children, as the living Christ, I want you to understand that I am not your salvation; I am simply a messenger of God's truth teachings. You are all to be the peacemakers. You are all to be your own salvation. You are all to hold the candle of light and to bring peace upon this planet. You are the peacekeepers and the way showers for this planet of love.

Dearest children, I am here to bring peace and love to any and all who will listen. Time is of the essence as there is no time to waste. Understand my teachings are for those who are ready to listen and ready to embrace their own divinity. Open your heart to love and use the violet flame of transformation, to transmute you own fear and pain into love. It is time to bring the energy of peace onto the world for humanity is now ready for peace to prevail upon planet Earth. You are the peacemakers and the way showers; therefore hold and carry peace where ever you go. Dearest children, walk in confidence with love, peace, and light within your heart. This energy of peace is a very powerful healing vibration that will heal the world. You are all the salvation for you are all children of peace, love and light. Allow yourself to embrace the energy of peace and understand the gift you bring upon the world is love. Hold and carry my essence and embody the energy of God within you. Go in peace. Go in love. Go in joy. I thank you.

And so, it is!

ʬ *Lesson of Joy* ऴ

Dearest children, it is I, Christ. I bring forth the final lesson, **Lesson XII: the Lesson of Joy**. Dearest children, it is time for each of you to embody the energy of joy and to no longer be affected by the negativity that exists in your physical plane. Joy is your birthright, just as the other eleven lessons are, as well. It is time for each of you to live in the essence of joy for simply, joy is the totality of all that there is. The vibration of joy is truly the last lesson, as it resonates to the frequency of God's love and light. Yes, it is true dearest children joy is the energy of God.

The lesson of joy is an important one as it resonates within the crystalline core of Mother Earth. At the very core of Mother Earth is where the purest essence of energy is held which is that direct connection to the love, light, peace and joy of the Great Creator. As each of you is connected to the vibrational frequency of joy, you are able to hold, within your physical presence, the essence of your divine spiritual self. As you allow this vibrational frequency of joy to bring peace, love, and hope within your heart, then there will be no fear or separation from your true divine self. When you feel joy, you are ecstatic. This is my message of the day: *live in joy and the remembrance of who you truly are*. Over time, these teachings have been forgotten. It is now time for your veils to be lifted. If you choose to awaken, you shall feel joy, peace, and love in their fullest essence and begin to emanate joy to the world. Dearest children, do not be afraid to bring love, joy, and peace onto the world. As each of you stand in the presence of God, awaken to the energy of joy. Feel the remembrance of *who you truly are*, as a joyous being of light.

Dearest children, remember to use the power of your breath and breathe in the energy of joy and allow this energy to resonate deep within your system. Allow the light of the Father to enter into your being in its fullest. You are the truth, the way, and the light. All of you are physical conduits holding the vibrational frequencies of joy, love, peace and light for this planet. The energy of joy is a powerful healing vibration which God has given you to *live in joy and remembrance of who you truly are*. Without joy there can be no hope and without hope there can be no joy. I have chosen joy to be the final lesson as it is the totality of all that is. Joy is the combination of all the truth teachings that holds the vibrational frequency of the number 13, the totality of all there is for this is the energy of God. All the <u>Twelve Mastery Teachings</u> are encoded with the power of love and the power of the Great I Am. The number 13 holds the powerful essence of God as all the Twelve Mastery Teachings are encoded with that same power.

Dearest children, as you begin to vibrate with the frequency of joy, you shall begin to use this energy within you for the greater good of mankind. Allow your heart to open to joy as I shall imprint this beautiful energy over your heart chakra. This imprint will awaken your cells and activate your every nuclei to respond to the energy of joy. As you begin to embrace this energy within you, allow it to resonate to every cell, every fiber, and every pore of your being. You were created in the image of the Great Creator and it is your right and your birthright to live in joy, as indeed you each are a god and a goddess. Allow yourself the gift of joy and embrace the energy in its fullest essence.

Dearest children, there is no need to live in fear or anger, but simply learn to live and embody joy in your daily life. You are a child of God and you are a child of the light. You are brothers and sisters of the light. You are the peacekeepers and the way showers, as you are the children who bring joy to the world. As you begin to radiate this, those in your presence will begin to feel the joy as it radiates from your system. The energy of joy has a resonance and a pulsation of its own frequency; just as the other eleven lessons do. These lessons are to be taught and to be shared with the masses to help humanity to awaken to God's truth teachings. Your birthright is love, power, truth, oneness, enlightenment, hope, faith, rejuvenation, remembrance, peace, and joy. As light workers it is your responsibility to help teach and lead the masses that we are all one and we are all connected. I, Christ, have imprinted joy within each of you on this day in order to remember your divine spiritual essence. If you choose to embrace this lesson of joy, it will lead you back home; for home is where the heart is and that is love. My truth teachings are resonating around the world for all to feel, for all to embody and to embrace within their physical essence. When you embrace and embody the frequency of joy, you will understand that living in this state is truly the peace that you have been looking for and you have, indeed, come home.

I, Christ, have chosen to share these truth teachings to help awaken humanity to their own divinity, so all can hold these twelve energies within them to embody the energy of peace that they desire. As you receive this gift God has given you to awaken to your true spiritual self, understand the responsibility it holds and carries, not only for yourself, but for the world at large. You are all one and you are all connected. You are all one with the divine Father and one with the divine Mother. No one is separate from another for you are all one, therefore, it is your responsibility to share and bring peace to your fellow brothers and sisters. As you embrace the energy of joy within you, then and only then, can you share this with the world around you. Each of you were created in the essence of love and light and as you embrace the circle of love and light that you were created from, then and only then can you feel God's light as it radiates light from your being. The vibrational frequency of joy is what others will see or sense in your presence. Some will feel it on a conscious level, and some may not feel it at all, but your light is shining brightly for those who choose to awaken.

When I lived on this planet over 2,000 years ago, I was taught these truth teachings which brought me great joy. I devoted my life to understanding God's principles so they could be understood and shared with the world. These teachings may sound simplistic, yet they are quite profound. Perhaps you do not understand the true meaning and essence of these teachings or how to embody them. It is by releasing the veil of forgetfulness that will awaken you to the true essence of my teachings. As your veils are being lifted, you tap into the essence of each of <u>The Twelve Mastery Teachings</u> through your own divine remembrance. This is a conscious decision each of you shall make. As you read these teachings, your veils are being lifted one-by-one-by-one. The totality of joy vibrates to the number 13, as it vibrates to the energy of God. This energy frees you and brings you back into balance and harmony. It is your responsibility to bring these vibrational frequencies into your physical essence as they were imprinted within you at your birth. All those who choose to receive these gifts will be activated as I speak. All you have to do is allow yourself to receive them and they are activated. The energy of joy vibrates at a power which increases the frequency within you, faster than speed of light. This vibrational frequency allows the energy of joy to pulsate from your own embodiment for all to see, all to feel, and, yes, all to know.

You are the children of the light who have chosen to embody and embrace these lessons and these truth teachings. Dearest children, I ask each of you to embrace and embody this **Lesson of Joy** within you in a sacred and responsible manner. My truth teachings are a part of the Great Design for the age of enlightenment as they are for all to receive on a conscious level. Dearest children, much has been given to you and much is being asked of you. If you so desire, I ask you to embrace these teachings in the responsible and sacred manner in which they were given. Today they have been imprinted within your soul and soul's essence and activated within your physical being through my words and through my presence as the Living Christ. As you allow joy and peace, to enter into your being allow the vibrational frequency of God's love to resonate throughout your essence. All of The Twelve Mastery Teachings shall begin to radiate from you. Embrace them and hold them as no other.

Dearest children, allow joy into your heart as the imprint of joy is forever imprinted within your system, your soul, and your soul's essence. It is imprinted within the essence of you being. It is your eternal birthright. Hold and carry this energy of totality of all that there is within you. Regardless of what you feel, regardless of your daily circumstances, hold and carry this energy of joy within you and you shall be brought back into balance and peace once again. My dearest children bring this energy of joy within your essence and know you are loved, you are at peace, and you are one with the Father. Joy to the world. Joy to the world. Joy to the world. Go in peace. And, above all, go in love. May you embrace my teachings as they were intended to be shared.

And so, it is!

❧ About the Author ☙

May the words of Christ fill
your heart with joy as it has mine!

Reverend Lea Chapin

Rev. Lea Chapin, MS; Ed holds a Master's of Science degree in counselor education and a Bachelor of Science degree in psychology. In addition, Rev. Lea became an Associate Pastor with the Church of the Creator. In 2004, Rev. Lea and her husband founded their own ministry, The Church of the White Light. Rev. Lea's ministry may be heard any time live on internet radio at www.RadioEarNetwork.com. She is the host of her own show, *Inspiration From Spirit*, which is broadcast on Tuesdays 3-4 PM EST, USA.

Rev. Lea has over 34 years as a spiritual counselor, teacher, medium, licensed massage therapist and energy healing practitioner. In 1993, Rev. Lea began to receive divinely inspired messages from the Ascended Masters and the Celestial/Angelic realm. Rev. Lea is a direct voice channel for the Ascended Masters and the Celestial Angelic. . Her work is uniquely empowering as it allows the soul and the subconscious to quickly heal and release all imprinted limiting beliefs and discordant energy that no longer serves. As our birthright we were designed to live in peace, harmony, joy, and balance in order to *live in joy and the remembrance of who we truly are.*

Both in-office and long distance spiritual consultations are available. For more information please call or email Rev. Lea to discuss what best fits your personal needs.

leachapin@verizon.net
www.CelestialConnections.biz

Made in United States
Orlando, FL
12 May 2022

17819499R00050